RECLAIMING THE PIAZZA II

Reclaiming the Piazza II
Catholic Education and the New Evangelisation

EDITED BY

RONNIE CONVERY
LEONARDO FRANCHI
RAYMOND McCLUSKEY

GRACEWING

First published in 2017 by
Gracewing
2 Southern Avenue
Leominster
Herefordshire HR6 0QF
United Kingdom
www.gracewing.co.uk

ISBN 978 085244 899 1

Typeset by Gracewing

Cover design by Stephen McPhee of Ipg Solutions Ltd, Glasgow

Contents

INTRODUCTION

T HE NEW EVANGELISATION (NE) is a long term project. There is no obvious short term 'fix' to the many and profound challenges facing the Catholic communities in the 'old' Christian lands.

To be effective, the energy of the NE must inform all aspects of the life of the Church. It cannot be another 'project' laid on top of, or alongside, the range of initiatives already in place. In light of this, we affirm in the present book that it is the family, as the primary cell of the Church (and of society), which must be at the centre of the NE. Alongside the family, the parish as community (confederation) of families, is called to form those who are attached, however loosely, to it.

Catholic education consists of both formal and informal processes. The formal aspect is found in the worldwide network of Catholic schools, colleges and universities which, in different and often challenging cultural contexts, offer education to people of all religious traditions and none. Informal education is not a second-rate set of educational processes but consists of countless initiatives in parishes and families designed to form people in virtue and religious knowledge.

Formal Catholic education, as described in the present book, is *a* centre of the NE, not *the* centre for the reason highlighted above. The Catholic school, for example, cannot, and should not, attempt to replace the family and parish as the principal nuclei of the life of the Church. The role of the Catholic school, in broad terms, is to live as an ecclesial body at the heart of the world. It is thus a uniquely privileged space, open to all but offering a vision which is distinctive. It therefore seems fitting to see the Catholic school, and by extension, the Catholic college and university, as a place where the NE can be explored and promoted.

The present volume brings together contributions from a range of people involved in the mission of Catholic education. It aims to offer food for thought on a conceptual level along with some more practical ideas regarding actual practice. The book is in two parts. In Part 1, we set out some of the big issues in the life of Catholic education. In Part 2, we present a series of personal (and often practical) reflections from key figures in the landscape of Catholic education. Taken together, we hope that both parts of the book offer a cohesive and accessible diet for prayer, reflection and study.

In Part 1 we explore some of the principal theoretical issues arising from the relationship between the New Evangelisation and Catholic Education. We are in the early years of the New Evangelisation and, as such, still developing our understanding of what it means for particular areas of the life of the Church. Education is one such area. The five essays in this section serve as markers for future debates on how to integrate thinking rooted in the mindset of the New Evangelisation into policy on Catholic education.

In Part 2 we offer some personal and practical insights on how the success of the New Evangelisation depends on the personal commitment and initiative of those who hold important offices in the Church's educational institutions. The roles highlighted in this section, while not exhaustive, offer focussed advice from people with experience in the front line, so to speak, of Catholic education. They speak from a personal perspective, thus putting in print that important 'craft wisdom' which is often needlessly diminished by those attached to overly theoretical understandings of education. The views expressed in the chapters are those of the individual authors and not necessarily of the editors.

ACKNOWLEDGEMENTS

A NY EDITED BOOK relies on the co-operation of those invited to contribute chapters. As editors we were delighted when all contributors promptly accepted the invitation to contribute to the book. We thank them for the dedication and patience they have shown in the lead up to publication.

We are indebted to Archbishop Rino Fisichella, President of the Pontifical Council for the Promotion of the New Evangelisation, for agreeing to write the Preface. We are very much honoured that, his very busy schedule notwithstanding, he agreed to contribute an overview of the New Evangelisation, the initiative to which he selflessly dedicates so much of his time. We are indebted to Mgr Graham Bell, Undersecretary at the Pontifical Council for the Promotion of the New Evangelisation, for his assistance in the preparation of the text.

We also thank Tom Longford of Gracewing for so readily agreeing to publish both this volume and its predecessor, *Reclaiming the Piazza: Catholic Education as a Cultural Project*, in 2014.

Ronnie Convery, Leonardo Franchi and Raymond McCluskey

FOREWORD

H EARING THE WORD of God lies at the heart of the New Evangelisation for it provides the ideal opportunity for an encounter with the person of Jesus Christ. Thus, the New Evangelisation calls for a renewed proclamation of the mystery of Christ's death and resurrection in order to bring about a reawakening of faith and a conversion of heart.

Since the day of Pentecost, the Church has never ceased responding to the Lord's command to proclaim the Gospel to all people. The content of this proclamation—the person of Jesus Christ, the Son of God—has never changed. What is 'new' and continues to develop is the form by which the one and the same Gospel *ab initio* is proclaimed with a fresh enthusiasm, in a contemporary and comprehensible language, with methodologies capable of transmitting the deepest sense of God's unchanging Word.

In the last decades, as the cacophonies of secularism, relativism, individualism, materialism, and indifference have continued to blare, many have become deaf to the Word of God and live without ever noticing the absence of God as a real absence in their lives. Yet, it is within this cultural context that Catholic schools and universities have the extraordinary opportunity to 'make the deaf hear' (Lk 7:22). For as Pope Francis affirms in his Apostolic Exhortation *Evangelii Gaudium*: 'Catholic schools, which always strive to join their work of education with the explicit proclamation of the Gospel, are a most valuable resource for the evangelisation of culture.'

Recognising the importance of Catholic education for the mission of the New Evangelisation requires that as a Church we earnestly and purposefully reflect upon the identity of Catholic educational institutions and their fundamental role in the New Evangelisation. We must understand better how these privileged places for the development of human thought and personal formation will become communities where critical thinking is encouraged, to allow each student to contribute meaningfully to the common good through the witness of his or her personal faith. The theoretical and practical contributions made by the authors of this book will serve as a helpful roadmap for this critical reflection.

The following pages provide those involved in the mission of Catholic schools and universities with the profound insights and concrete applications necessary for establishing academic institutions as dynamic centres of proclamation. The urgency of such centres was underscored by Pope Francis in his message to the Members of the Congregation for Catholic Education: 'Catholic schools and universities are equally called to offer to all the Christian message—respecting fully the freedom of all and the proper methods of each specific scholastic environment—namely that Jesus Christ is the meaning of life, of the cosmos and of history.'

As we survey the many challenges faced along the path of the New Evangelisation, we must remember that we do not travel this route alone. In our Catholic schools and universities, there are administrators, teachers, support-staff, parents, and students who walk this path with us, offering the company of faith, and inspiring each other with reasons to believe. The time is at hand to regain the credibility of our Catholic educational institutions, and to demonstrate that they are indeed capable of responding to the difficulties of today by sending forth into the world graduates who are, as we read in Matthew 5:13–14, salt of the earth, lights of the world, and cities set on a hill.

✠ Rino Fisichella
Titular Archbishop of Vicohabentia
President
Pontifical Council for the Promotion of the New Evangelisation

PART 1

CATHOLIC EDUCATION AND THE NEW EVANGELISATION: THEORETICAL REFLECTIONS

EXPLAINING THE NEW EVANGELISATION

Archbishop Leo Cushley

In principio erat verbum

Motto of St Mary's College, University of St Andrews

THE ESTABLISHMENT OF St Mary's College in the university city of St Andrews was one of the last acts of Archbishop James Beaton (c.1473–1539). In fact, he died just days after its official inauguration. In gaining approval for its foundation from Pope Paul III the year previous, Archbishop Beaton aspired to form and foster a better educated clergy in order to counter the new religious ideas of Martin Luther sweeping into Scotland from Germany. The founding Papal Bull describes the establishment of:

> a College of clerics, scholars and presbyters with a church or chapel under the invocation of the Blessed Virgin Mary, for the teaching of grammar, logic, natural philosophy, theology and medicine, canon and civil law, with the right to grant its own degrees.[1]

Beaton's attempt at Counter-Reformation failed and St Mary's subsequently became the home to the university's Divinity faculty. It now shares its historic quadrangle, graced with a thorn tree planted by Mary, Queen of Scots, with the university's School of Psychology and Neuroscience, as well as the Department of Biology.

Like nearly all other St Andrews undergraduates, the scientists wear red academic gowns. Uniquely, the divines are permitted to wear black gowns embellished with a purple saltire. All students, though, arrive for classes at St Mary's Quad through the same stone archway where is to be found that college motto cast in wrought iron above the entrance gates.

In principio erat verbum is, of course, drawn from the first line of the Gospel of St John: 'In the beginning was the Word.' As any of the budding biblical scholars at St Mary's will tell you, however, the original Greek is λόγος or *Logos* from which 'Word' is the most plausible English derivation.

Logos, though, would have resonated in the ear of the Hellenic world of the second century with greater profundity than 'Word' does within the Anglosphere of the twenty-first century. From the time of Heraclitus of Ephesus in the sixth century BC, the term *Logos* had developed among many Greek philosophers to denote the principle of order or knowledge in the Universe. 'All entities come to be in accordance with this *Logos*,' said Heraclitus himself.[2] Thus the incarnation of Jesus Christ as encapsulated by Saint John — also, most likely, of Ephesus — assumes heightened historic significance; the Word, the Logos, became flesh and dwelt among us. If this is true, then all academic disciplines should find their meaning in Christ. Not just theology but also psychology, neuroscience and biology too. Black gowns as well as red. Faith as well as science. All things renewed in Christ. God as all in all.

And yet, we know this not to be the intellectual instinct of the society within which most of our young people live and learn, both at university and school. Why? And does it matter? Let's travel from South Street in St Andrews to the Royal Mile in Edinburgh to answer both those questions.

There, within less than a couple of hundred yards of each other, you will find two rather handsome neo-classical statues, both the creation of the Paisley-based sculptor Sandy Stoddart.[3] In front of the High Court sits David Hume; just down the street, beyond St Giles' Cathedral, is Adam Smith. The lives of these two great figures of the eighteenth century Scottish Enlightenment tell us much about when and how contemporary society began to develop a common mindset of practical agnosticism and a binary assumption as regards faith and science.

Born within a dozen years of each other, David Hume (1711–1776) and Adam Smith (1723–1790) were baptised and brought up within the presbyterian Church of Scotland. As it happens, both also grew up fatherless. As a boy, Hume attended his local kirk in Berwickshire where his uncle was the minister. He later recalled that he was 'religious when he was young' and had even taken to contrasting his youthful vices and virtues against the moral guidelines set out in the Calvinistic devotional work, *The Whole Duty of Man*.[4]

Adam Smith's father had belonged to the moderate wing of the Church of Scotland. There is even a suggestion that Smith himself may have considered a career as a cleric—he won a Snell Exhibition scholarship to Balliol College, University of Oxford, traditionally awarded under bond to take Anglican orders and return to Scotland—but his 1790 obituary in *The Times* noted that 'the Church seemed an improper profession, because he had early become a disciple of Voltaire in matters of religion.'[5]

These two men—David Hume and Adam Smith—met in 1750 and remained great friends until Hume's death 26 years later. They lived at a time when open dissent from the orthodoxies of the Scots Kirk could carry serious consequences, both professionally and personally. The execution of the last man in Scotland condemned for blasphemy, 20-year-old student Thomas Aikenhead, took place in Edinburgh in 1697, only a decade and a half prior to Hume's birth. Therefore, the precise religious views of both have been debated ever since.

Certainly, Smith was a church-going Presbyterian and upon becoming Chair of Logic at the University of Glasgow in 1751 signed the Calvinist Westminster Confession of Faith before the Glasgow Presbytery. His *Theory of Moral Sentiments*, published 1759, is also seemingly underpinned by an assumption of a divine economy at work within creation. For example, 'every part of nature, when attentively surveyed, equally demonstrates the providential care of its Author, and we may admire the wisdom and goodness of God even in the weakness and folly of man.'[6]

However, the language he employs is largely drawn from that eighteenth century Deist lexicon: 'the Deity', 'the Author of nature', 'the great Director of nature' and so on. In fact, in his now better known *Wealth of Nations*, published in 1776, Smith doesn't deploy the term 'God' or 'Author of nature' at all, and 'the Deity' only twice. Therefore, in the works of Smith we can perhaps observe a generational shift in emphasis, typical of the Enlightenment, regarding the Creator's interplay with creation. God as transcendent, yes. God as immanent, somewhat. God as incarnate, little to no comment.

As with many matters, David Hume is more clear cut. Whatever the precise opinion Hume held regarding God, it was certainly one that viewed any possible Creator as distant and indifferent to the created order. For Hume, God was 'a Being, so remote and incomprehensible, who bears much less analogy to any other being in the universe than the sun to a waxen taper' as he states in his 1748 *An Enquiry Concerning Human Understanding.*[7]

Hume conjectured that God can be perceived 'only by some faint traces or outlines' beyond which 'we have no authority to ascribe to him any attribute or perfection.'

Thus, where the presence of the incarnate God was once very tangible within the day-to-day life of a Christendom suffused with sacraments and sacramentals, now the Creator seemed to be retreating from his creatures to exist behind a veil of celestial indifference.

Also contained within the writings of Smith, and even more so Hume, we can witness the Enlightenment's departure away from the medieval assumption that all fields of academic learning, including the sciences, fell harmoniously within the orbit of St Augustine's maxim, *Credo ut intellegam, intellego ut credam.*[8]

'Science is the great antidote to the poison of enthusiasm and superstition,' writes Smith in his *Wealth of Nations*, suggesting that modern science was engaged in an historic joust with religion to provide humanity with an explanation of the 'great phenomena of nature':

> Superstition first attempted to satisfy this curiosity, by referring all those wonderful appearances to the immediate agency of the gods. Philosophy afterwards endeavoured to account for them from more familiar causes, or from such as mankind were better acquainted with, than the agency of the gods.'[9]

Similarly, Hume gives short shrift to the schoolmen of medieval Europe stating that 'Scholastic learning and polemical divinity retarded the growth of all true knowledge,' in *The History of England* (1754–61).[10] Thus, where a synthesis of religion and reason was once presumed, there emerged an assumption of polarity. Over the past two centuries, it is this notion which has proliferated through most seats of learning in the West.

In fact, the intellectual lineage of the Enlightenment is such that the vast majority of our young people are now born into a society where such modernist or, more often, postmodernist nostrums permeate the cultural air they breathe: there is no ultimate purpose, no objective truth or, if there is, we can neither perceive nor grasp it. Not surprisingly, in response many young people recuse themselves from the search for life's essential meaning, settling instead for a dizzying tinsel show of distractions that can sometimes bring a moment's satisfaction but all too often leaves the youthful soul unhappy and unsatisfied. Indeed, the anecdotal and statistical evidence suggests that the ever-enveloping culture of 'debonair nihilism'[11] gives our young people little reason to laugh or even, sometimes, to live. So, what is to be done? In search of an answer, let us continue our stroll down Edinburgh's Royal Mile until we arrive at the ancient Palace of Holyroodhouse.

It was there on the morning of Thursday, 16 September 2010 that Benedict XVI began the first ever state visit by a reigning Pope to the United Kingdom. Standing next to Her

Majesty, Queen Elizabeth, the 83-year-old German pontiff acknowledged the common wartime history shared with the 84-year-old British monarch:

> As we reflect on the sobering lessons of the atheist extremism of the twentieth century, let us never forget how the exclusion of God, religion and virtue from public life leads ultimately to a truncated vision of man and of society and thus to a reductive vision of the person and his destiny.[12]

As it happens, I was just yards away from the Pope as he offered his insights to the invited guests gathered on the palace lawn at the rear of Holyroodhouse. Standing there, I recalled how, for many months, most of Britain's leading media outlets had predicted the Papal Visit to the UK would meet with deep disinterest or, even, doom. And yet, as Pope Benedict departed the palace, draped in his bespoke papal tartan, it became apparent that the pundits had again misjudged the mood of the populace. In total, an estimated 125,000 people lined the streets of Edinburgh as the Popemobile slowly made its way through the Scottish capital. Such scenes were soon repeated in Glasgow, London and Birmingham.

So why did people turn out? Yes, some were there to cheer, others merely to witness the public spectacle, but it became very apparent that, primarily, the people of Britain were coming to listen. Upon closer inspection, 'God's Rottweiler', as the UK press had previously labelled Pope Benedict, turned out to be a kindly, soft-spoken German intellectual, who was willing to listen, engage and dialogue with all the doubts, fears and questions that the modern mind has regarding ultimate realties but is often too afraid to ask, usually due to that aforementioned post-modern presumption that no definitive answers are to be had.

'The Catholic tradition maintains that the objective norms governing right action are accessible to reason, prescinding from the content of revelation,'[13] proposed Pope Benedict to an eminent cross-section of British civil society gathered in Westminster Hall, 17 September 2010, before setting out the case for the mutual reliance of reason upon religion, and vice-versa, within any properly functioning polity.

> This is why I would suggest that the world of reason and the world of faith—the world of secular rationality and the world of religious belief—need one another and should not be afraid to enter into a profound and ongoing dialogue, for the good of our civilization.

In that moment, it was obvious to all of us present in Westminster Hall that the ancient faith of England, older even than the great medieval hammerbeam roof above us there, was being appraised afresh by many among the country's great and good who had, perhaps, intellectually folded away Christianity with the things of childhood. In that moment, I would suggest, we may have been witness to a turning point, a significant staging post on the path towards a new evangelisation within the British Isles and beyond. Here was the common language of reason being intelligently employed to propose a coherent, compelling and compassionate re-presentation of the person of Jesus Christ to the intellectual classes of the West, who historically have been shaped by Christianity but who have slowly drifted away from the *credo* and custom of the Faith in recent centuries.

As with civil society, so with our schools. If there is to be a new evangelisation fostered within Catholic education, it has to go beyond the confines of the Religious Education department and, instead, should aspire to make Jesus Christ the cornerstone of any contemporary curriculum.

'Christianity must always remember that it is the religion of the *Logos*. It is faith in the *Creator Spiritus*, in the Creator Spirit, from which proceeds everything that exists,'[14] said the then Cardinal Ratzinger at Subiaco near Rome in April 2005, the day prior to Pope Saint John Paul II's death. The location of the discourse was both providential and, for our purpose here, instructive.

It was in Subiaco in the early sixth century, that a young Saint Benedict began to live a hermitical life after turning his back on the dissolute ways of post-imperial Rome. Three years of solitude, prayer and study then followed before he emerged to establish, in total, a dozen monasteries in the vicinity of Subiaco and, subsequently, the great monastery at Monte Cassino. Western monasticism was thus born. At the same time, the end of the Roman Empire gave way to darker and less certain times in Europe. It was amid that cultural gloom that the monasteries—and the communities that grew up around them—shone ever brighter as beacons of civility and learning. Eventually, it was these saintly scholars, or scholarly saints, who set forth to convert, or reconvert, Europe and create a new civilisation, Christendom, that held fast for a thousand years. That was the original evangelisation of Europe. Today, each and every Catholic school is called to be its own little Subiaco, each fostering a new civilisation of virtue, reason and learning rooted in Jesus Christ.

'Only creative reason, which in the crucified God is manifested as love, can really show us the way,' added Cardinal Ratzinger in Subiaco:

> In the very necessary dialogue between secularists and Catholics, we Christians must be very careful to remain faithful to this fundamental line: to live a faith that comes from the *Logos*, from creative reason, and that, because of this, is also open to all that is truly rational.[15]

Of course, we can never impose Christ upon our young people, nor would we ever want to, but we can and should propose Christ as the *Logos* who can make greatest sense of all our academic studies and, indeed, of our lives too. The model for that endeavour has traditionally been the Magi, those wise men of the ancient East, who allowed themselves to be guided by reason and science and, in doing so, found their way to the Christ Child, the *Logos* incarnate.

There is one further, specific challenge that the New Evangelisation brings for Catholic teachers: the imperative to strive for unity of life. What I mean is this: as with anybody privileged enough to proclaim the Gospel, our words and actions have to be consonant, one with the other. After all, Jesus Christ is not only the Truth, he is also the Way and the Life. Orthodoxy requires orthopraxy and that requires a serious-minded pursuit of holiness, the fullness of Christian life, in the midst of the world. As Pope Francis said during a memorable audience in November 2014:

> It is by living with love and offering Christian witness in our daily tasks that we are called to become saints ... Yes, you can! There, where you work you can become a saint. God gives you the grace to become a saint. God communicates with you. Always and everywhere you can become a saint, that is, by being receptive to the grace that is working in us and leads us to holiness.[16]

This, however, can only happen when our interior life is nurtured by private prayer. There is no other starting point, no other route. It is only private prayer that will lead to grounded public prayer that will lead to a Catholic ethos that fosters a new evangelisation.

The result will be Catholic teachers who live lives of servant leadership modelled upon Jesus Christ himself. Just as he astonished the crowd by teaching 'as one who had authority, and not as their scribes,' our young people will also detect the difference.[17] They too have a nose for the authentic as opposed to the ersatz.

A final thought. Edinburgh's Royal Mile, the location for much of our intellectual expedition thus far, is topped and tailed by two important places of worship. At the lower end, there are the ruins of the priory of the Augustinians, now in the lawn of Holyroodhouse; and at the top, there is the oldest extant building in Edinburgh, St Margaret's chapel at the heart of Edinburgh Castle. These Christian bookends of the Royal Mile have seen many vicissitudes for their Christian culture and civilisation. Much has been achieved by Christian men and women in their shadow, and much has been lost. These buildings, tokens of the past, are now visited as curiosities by believer and non-believer alike. Their builders meant to raise minds and hearts to God, the better to love the Almighty and serve their neighbour; while those who erected statues to Hume and Smith wished to honour men committed to informing their fellows and improving their lot. At their best, these are all people who wish to see humanity bettered. And as for our own times and people? Like our noble (Scots) forebears in philosophy, the arts and the sciences, we too ought to be able to identify and to grasp the opportunities afforded us, to explore with our fellows the great questions that face all the human beings that will ever live: why *are* we here? What *ought* we to do with our life? And, as we share much in our common mortality, there surely needs to be a public space where the perennial questions of human existence are aired without prejudice or rancour. After all, in the eighteenth century David Hume maintained an amiable dialogue with John Gordon, Catholic priest and Principal of the Scots College in Paris. Similarly, in the twentieth century, Cardinal Ratzinger engaged in robust but respectful public discussion with neo-Marxist philosopher Jürgen Habermas.[18] Perhaps in the twenty-first century, we need a new Royal Mile, where truth and charity walk and talk hand in hand, to the benefit of all those participating in the conversation.

Notes

1   Taken from St Andrews University website article marking 475 years of St Mary's College. Available at www.st-andrews.ac.uk/news/archive/2013/title,199484,en.php.

2   See H. A. Shapiro (ed.), *The Cambridge Companion to Archaic Greece* (Cambridge: Cambridge University Press, 2007).

3   Alexander 'Sandy' Stoddart (1959–) is a Scottish sculptor, who, since 2008, has been the Queen's Sculptor in Ordinary in Scotland. He works primarily on figurative sculpture in clay within the neoclassical tradition. He is based in Paisley, a town in the west of Scotland.

4   D. Hume, *A Treatise of Human Nature*, Vol. 2, edited by D. F. Norton

and M. J. Norton, (Oxford: Oxford University Press, 2007).

5   E. Rothschild, *Economic Sentiments: Adam Smith, Concordet and the Enlightenment*, (Cambridge, MA: Harvard University Press, 2013).

6   A. Smith, 'Of the Final Cause of this Irregularity of Sentiments' in *The Theory of Moral Sentiments* (Gutenberg Publishers, 1759/2011).

7   D. Hume, *An Enquiry Concerning Human Understanding* (Simon & Brown, 1748/2011).

8   See St Augustine of Hippo, *Tract on the Gospel of John* 29:6 and St Anselm, *Proslogion*, 1. 'I believe in order to understand; I understand in order to believe.'

9   A. Smith, *The Wealth of Nations: Books I-III* (1776) (London: Penguin Books, 1982).

10   D. Hume, *The History of England from the Invasion of Julius Caesar to the Revolution of 1688*, vol. 6, (London: T. Cadell, 1782), p. 197.

11   See A. Bloom, *The Closing of the American Mind* (New York: Simon & Schuster, 1987).

12   Pope Benedict XVI, *Address at Palace of Holyroodhouse*, Edinburgh, 16 September 2010.

13   Pope Benedict XVI, Address at meeting with the Representatives of British Society, including the Diplomatic Corps, Politicians, Academics and Business Leaders, Westminster Hall, London, 17 September 2010.

14   Translation of the lecture given in Italian by Cardinal Joseph Ratzinger, now Pope Emeritus Benedict XVI, in the convent of Saint Scholastica in Subiaco, Italy, upon reception of the St Benedict Award for the promotion of life and the family in Europe, 1 April 2005. Available at: http://www.catholiceducation.org/ en/culture/catholic-contributions/cardinal-ratzinger-on-europe-s-crisis-of-culture.html.

15   *Ibid.*

16   Pope Francis, *Address at General Audience*, 19 November 2014.

17   Mt 7:28–29.

18   Cardinal Ratzinger and Jürgen Habermas were in public discussion on 19 January, 2004, at a debate hosted by the Bavarian Catholic Academy on the topic of 'Pre-political moral foundations in the construction of a free civil society, with specific reference to the democratic constitutional state.' See J. Habermas and J. Ratzinger, *The Dialectics of Secularization: On Reason and Religion* (San Francisco: Ignatius Press, 2006).

CATHOLIC EDUCATION AS A THEOLOGICAL PROJECT

Tracey Rowland

A NYONE WHO HAS ever taught children in a Catholic school or taught young undergraduates in Catholic tertiary institutions, has had an experience of spiritual fatherhood or motherhood. Catholics, better than anyone, understand that education is not primarily or even predominately about supplying members of the workforce with market-driven skills. That was the Soviet idea of education and it is also, somewhat ironically, an idea about which there is strong agreement between Marxists and free market economists. Both have a tendency to think of education as a process to produce 'human resources' for the labour market.

Of course, Catholic educators do want their students to be employable and otherwise be useful members of their communities, but the point I wish to emphasise in this chapter is that the Catholic vision of education is fundamentally theological not economic.[1]

The German Romantics of the nineteenth century and many educational theorists today talk about the concept of *Bildung*. This is sometimes translated as education, but more often, as self-cultivation or self-development. The general idea is that education is about the formation of the human character or human 'self' or 'soul'.

What I wish to argue in this chapter is that Catholic education is a specific form of *Bildung* governed by the maxim that we have been made in the Image of God, to grow into the likeness of Christ. A Catholic vision of education as a theological project is built upon a Catholic theological anthropology, including the idea that Christ is the Way, the Truth and the Life, as the motto of the University of Glasgow acclaims.

A foundational principle of Catholic cosmology is that everything in creation has been marked by the form of the Trinity. Trinitarian relationships abound in nature as mathematicians, physicists and botanists tell us. Most important of all are the marks of the Trinity in human nature. There is the highly important Trinitarian relationship between activities of the human soul, such as thinking, remembering and willing and the theological virtues of faith, hope and love, and the transcendental properties of being, namely, truth, beauty and goodness. The Trinitarian scheme can become even more complex when we bring in the transcendental property of unity and the human imagination, and the seven gifts of the Holy Spirit—wisdom, understanding, counsel, knowledge, fortitude, piety and fear of the Lord—with each gift targeted on the correct operation of one of the activities of the soul.

At the base of any Catholic understanding of education there is the idea that there exists a relationship between the human intellect, the theological virtue of faith, and the transcendental of truth; there also exists a relationship between the human will, the theological virtue of love, and the transcendental of goodness, and there exists a relationship between the human memory, the theological virtue of hope and the transcendental of beauty.

To produce graduates from Catholic educational institutions who actually have the Catholic faith and practise it, one needs, therefore, to pay close attention to the development of these relationships in the formation of one's students. At the end of the day, after some twelve years in a Catholic educational system, one needs to be able to say that one's graduates have Catholic intellects, Catholic wills, Catholic imaginations, and Catholic memories all working in tandem and brought into a coherent symphony by a Catholic heart.

A Catholic intellect is interested in truth, a Catholic is interested in goodness and has been trained to fight concupiscence through various ascetic practices of self-denial in the penitential seasons of Lent and Advent. A Catholic imagination is one that can grasp ideas presented mytho-poetically. J. R. R. Tolkien and C. S Lewis were two of the two greatest writers of the twentieth century with mytho-poetic imaginations. Tolkien was a Catholic and Lewis asymptotically approached a Catholic vision. A child with a well-developed Catholic imagination will have no trouble identifying Aslan with Christ. A young woman with a Catholic imagination should have no trouble understanding Archbishop Javier Martinez's statement that she should never accept a marriage proposal from any man who has not first presented her with the corpse of at least three dragons! A Catholic memory is a memory filled with knowledge of the great moments in salvation history, including a store of knowledge about the lives of the saints and the struggles of the Church in previous centuries. A Catholic memory should also include a store of liturgical experiences, in a manner analogous to the experience of the Apostles of Christ's Transfiguration. All of these various activities of the human soul need to be nurtured to increase their receptivity to grace and to help them to participate in all that is true, and beautiful and good.

The American Franciscan psychologist, the late Fr Benedict Groeschel, was of the view that each person has a primary attraction to one or other of the transcendentals, that is, to truth, beauty or goodness. This is a bit like a Catholic theory of personality types. The famous Myers-Briggs personality type test looks at issues such as whether a person is primarily an introvert or an extrovert, primarily a thinking type or a feeling type, primarily an intuitive type or someone more attuned to concrete details, and finally, someone who likes to get a job done or alternatively, someone who likes to dream about the best way to approach the job before actually getting on and doing it. There is value in this type of analysis so long as one does not overplay its significance and tie people down with labels from which they can never escape, but Fr Groeschel supplements this kind of analysis with the idea that some of us are just made with a stronger appetite or aptitude for one or other of the transcendentals. Some of us are the truth types for whom the intellectual clarity of the faith is a great source of wonder and consolation. Others, the more heart-centred types, are more into goodness, and thus the virtues, and yet others, the strong artistic personality types, are attracted to the beauty of the Church, especially to the splendour of her liturgy. Groeschel offered St. Thomas Aquinas as an example of the first type, St Francis of Assisi as an example of the second type, and St Augustine as an example of the third type. However any saint worthy of the name is attracted to all three transcendentals, to truth, beauty and goodness, and is strong in all the theological virtues, that is, has large reserves of faith, hope and love, and thus fully functional intellects, memories and wills.

Conversely, those of us who are not saints can have our spiritual pathologies diagnosed by reference to the weak operation of one or other of the theological virtues in our souls. Are we low on faith, on hope or love, or anaemic in all three areas, do we care about truth, about goodness or about beauty? Some people care about one transcendental but not the others. Thus, as a caricature, we have the priggish nerd types who can brag about having read every papal encyclical since Leo XIII but are not really kind or patient or sympathetic, in short, not really all that loving. Then there are the aesthetes who love solemn liturgy but care little about moral theology and can be quite uncharitable about people who sing badly or who lack knowledge of liturgical rubrics. There are also the 'all you need is love' types who are a bit dippy and regard Church teachings on doctrinal matters as completely irrelevant. They are the people whom Cardinal Pell describes as believers in the Donald Duck heresy, the heresy which says that since my intentions were good, the act itself was good, even if inconsistent with the Ten Commandments or other biblical teachings. There are also people who have been infected with the Calvinist fear of beauty. For Calvinists, beauty is a Greek concern which illegitimately crept into the Christian tradition via the works of St Augustine. Calvinists and common garden variety seventeenth-century British puritans didn't want Christianity to be tied to beauty. They went about smashing altars and otherwise demanding an architectural and liturgical austerity, and various Puritan forms of dress. These attitudes were sadly fostered in the Catholic community by the Jansenist heresy and in more recent times by some schools of liberation theology according to which an interest in beauty is regarded as a middle class or worse, aristocratic fetish.

This is of course a caricature of human types, and most people are not such extreme cases, but I mention these more extreme types to help make concrete what Fr Groeschel meant when he spoke of primary transcendentals. The point is that in all Catholic educational institutions, people should be interested in truth, in goodness and in beauty, and they need to understand the importance of faith, hope and love for the activities of the human soul, since it is these virtues which assist the soul's receptivity to truth, to beauty and to goodness. For those of you who want to explore this topic further, I would recommend Fr Groeschels' book *Spiritual Passages* and Pope Benedict's encyclicals on love and hope and the first encyclical of Pope Francis which was on faith. The encyclical on faith was drafted by Pope Benedict and completes his suite of encyclicals on the theological virtues. The Irish Dominican, Fr Vincent McNabb addressed the importance of beauty and truth in the following statement:

> Into the great Temple of Truth, the Church of God, there are two gates — the gate of wisdom and the gate of beauty. I am inclined to think that the narrow gate is the gate of wisdom, and the wide gate, though which millions pass, is the gate of beauty. The Catholic Church has these portals ever open. She welcomes from time to time the few philosophers and thinkers who crucify themselves by thought, but

> she welcomes unceasingly the countless numbers
> who come for her colour, for her song, for her
> smile—as they go afield for the warmth and light of
> the Spring sun.[2]

Conversely, Gerhard Nebel, a twentieth-century Protestant
theologian who studied under Martin Heidegger, observed:

> Anyone who is concerned with the world in all its
> range, with forms and proportions, with man's
> heroism, with morality, with the splendor of forms,
> with the exploration of the sphere of myth, will feel
> repelled by Protestantism. Luther destroyed the rich
> treasury of myth, and replaced it with an arid,
> official Institute. Anyone enamored of beauty will
> shiver in the barn of the Reformation, just as Winck-
> elmann did, and feel the pull of Rome.[3]

Nebel had recognised the Protestant hostility to beauty and
was trying from within the Protestant academic community
to remedy the pathology.

Those who have been influenced by the Montessori
pedagogy developed for catechetical purposes by Sofia
Cavalletti, are of the view that one must begin with the
concrete and hence things that are beautiful, then move onto
the affective level, and finally bring in the intellectual
analysis and doctrine after the heart has been right-ordered.
In the earliest stages of a child's education liturgy is
extremely important because the liturgy is something both
concrete and beautiful.

As a generalisation it is said that pre-Conciliar religious
education, influenced by neo-scholasticism, had a tendency
to be truth first and intellect-dominant which was sometimes very effectively supplemented by the personal
witness of religious who addressed the more affective needs
of children, but in the absence of inspirational religious who
concretely embodied the ideas presented, the material was
often difficult for students to internalise. After the Council
there was a tendency to swing toward giving priority to the

affective and to down-play the intellectual with equally unsatisfactory results.

The approach of the Cavalletti school of catechesis and religious education, which includes the popular Good Shepherd programme which is currently promoted throughout the world by Mother Theresa's Missionaries of Charity, starts with the concrete and liturgical and leads up to the intellectual. The youngest children begin their cate-chetical formation by being presented with a model city of Jerusalem, complete with camels and palm trees, the temple, the Mount of Olives, the Garden of Gethsemane, King Herod's palace, the via dolorosa and so on. Later they move on to play with model altars and liturgical vessels, learning the names for each part of a Church and each vessel and each cloth for use on an altar. The purpose of this is to stimulate their imaginations and to help them to have a concrete understanding of things which they will later understand at a more abstract intellectual level.

Thus while there is no 'one size fits all' blue-print for the effective Catholic education of children because each child is unique with different aptitudes and personality strengths and weaknesses, nonetheless, as a generalisation one can conclude that educators do need to be mindful of the fact that the children in their care have imaginations that need to be stimulated, have rational intellects thirsting for answers to the fundamental questions about the meaning of human life, have hearts that need to learn about love and have memories that need a good store of 'sapiential experiences', that is, experiences of love and beauty and goodness.

A problem we have had with many catechetical pro-grammes is that they are designed to overcome a defect in a previous catechetical programme and so we have tended to lurch from a lop-sided emphasis on doctrine to a lop-sided emphasis on the affective dimensions, from a focus on truth to a focus on goodness, but never quite getting it altogether because to get it altogether we have to simultaneously pay attention to a number of the soul's activities, to three theological virtues and to three transcendental properties. It is like conducting an orchestra where all the relationships between the component parts exist in a Trinitarian, or to use the theological term, perichoretic, or circular-dance style relationship. If one of the component parts is drowned out or overlooked, the other component parts are weakened. Just as it is the *relationships* within the Holy Trinity that are all important for understanding the God-head, it is the relationships between the various activities of the human soul that are important for the development of a person's character. Human lives can turn into narrative wrecks if educators produce people who can think at high levels of abstraction but are emotionally retarded or who lack sapiential experiences, or who, conversely, are emotionally sensitive but have no intellectual framework with which to make judgments about their inner life.

It is also important that students understand that the Christian God is a Trinitarian God. This might sound so obvious as to be ridiculous but I have certainly come across many graduates of Catholic schools who are, theologically speaking, 'anonymous unitarians'. Immanual Kant famously said that whether there are ten persons in the deity, or 3, it makes no difference. Kant was not however a Catholic.

Early in his academic career Karl Rahner complained that not enough attention was given to the Trinity in Catholic theology academies. Theologians of the Vatican II generation like Yves Congar tried to fill this gap with studies on the significance of the Holy Spirit.

St. John Paul II also began his pontificate by publishing a suite of three encyclicals on the subject of the Trinity — each one dealt with a distinct Person of the Trinity and how that Person works in the economy of human salvation. *Redemptor Hominis*, published in 1979, examined the relationship between each human person and God the Son, *Dives in Misericordia* published in 1980 looked at how God the Son reveals God the Father to humanity, and incidentally in the Year of Mercy, this particular encyclical furnished an extensive analysis of the theology of mercy which was a subject close to the heart of St John Paul II; and finally, the encyclical *Dominum et vivificantem* published in 1986, looked at how God the Holy Spirit universalises the redemptive work of Christ so that it may reach each person.

In order to put together a Catholic anthropology one can therefore combine the insights to be found in Pope St John Paul's trilogy of encyclicals on the Trinity with Pope Benedict's trilogy of encyclicals on the theological virtues.

To conclude this section, one can say that a hallmark of a Catholic concept of *Bildung* or character-formation is its Christocentric Trinitarianism. Whether one is teaching 5 year olds at an Infants' School, or teenagers in a secondary school or adults in a Catholic university, the same theological anthropology is operative.

Sadly however, this Christocentric Trinitarianism is often not well understood because subjects on theological anthropology rarely form part of the curriculum for the formation of catechists and others entrusted with the religious education of children. It is not that people are opposed to Trinitarian anthropology, it is rather that they often know nothing about it.

Self-Secularising Practices

Often people will speak of Catholic values or Christian values and it is common for non-Catholics to say that Catholic schools have 'good values' by which they mean that such schools are places where students are encouraged to be kind and tolerant of others less intelligent or less athletically competent than themselves. They mean that there is often less bullying behaviour at Catholic schools. This is true and a good thing, but there is a danger here that in this era of political correctness and outright intolerance of faith traditions, people are tempted to separate these desirable values from Christ himself. To use a brewing metaphor there is the temptation to distil the Christian values from Christ and to offer the world a package of values stripped of the need for any personal relationship with Christ. When Pope Benedict used the expression 'self-secularisation' he was referring to this kind of practice—the attempt to offer the world so-called Christian values detached or distilled from a personal belief in Christ and participation in the sacramental life of the Church which is one of the most powerful ways in which God communicates with his creatures.

A prominent Catholic scholar who understands the problem of this self-secularising temptation is Alasdair MacIntyre. MacIntyre was born in Glasgow, the son of two doctors who were both graduates of the University of Glasgow. One parent was a Catholic and one was from the 'Wee Frees' tradition. MacIntyre has attributed his understanding of the philosophy of culture to his early childhood immersion in what he described as being four different cultures—that of Scottish Catholicism, that of Wee Frees Calvinism, that of the Gaelic speaking west coast islands and that of an Anglicised intellectual milieu. Having a childhood immersion in four different cultural communities helped him to understand how ideas are transmitted through social practices as much as through intellectual propositions, and how even our understanding of intellectual propositions is highly dependent upon our linguistic traditions. In particular he understood how hard it is to transpose ideas from one dialect to another. These early childhood experiences and intuitions have made MacIntyre into a world-class Catholic philosopher and an authority on the problem of the secularisation of formerly Christian cultures. As early as 1953 in his book *Marxism: An Interpretation*, he wrote:

> When the sacred and the secular are divided, then religion becomes one more department of human life, one activity among others... This has in fact happened in bourgeois religion... Only a religion which is a way of living in every sphere either deserves to or can hope to survive. For the task of

religion is to help see the secular as the sacred, the world as under God. When the sacred and the secular are separated, then the natural becomes an end, not the hallowing of the world, but in itself... To divide the sacred from the secular is to recognise God's action only within the narrowest of limits. A religion which recognises such a division... is one on the point of dying.[4]

In other words, pragmatically motivated projects to distil Christian values from a personal relationship to God and participation in the sacramental life of the Church, for reasons such as the promotion of social harmony or accommodation to government policies, will always end in the marginalisation of God and the self-secularisation of the institutions in which such strategies are fostered.

Those who work in the field of tertiary education may well be familiar with MacIntyre's book *God, Philosophy, Universities: A Selective History of the Catholic Philosophical Tradition.*[5] In this work MacIntyre makes three substantial arguments:

1. that one cannot make any sense of the contemporary culture wars within Western society without some knowledge of contending philosophical systems;

2. that contemporary philosophical and cultural conflict cannot be understood outside the intellectual and social history of its development, so that a knowledge of the current state of play in any given conflict is not sufficient—one needs to understand the intellectual and social history that precedes the current state of play and

3. that philosophy is not 'just a matter of propositions affirmed or denied and of arguments advanced and critically evaluated, but of philosophies in particular social and cultural situations interacting with each other in their affirmations and demand',

so that the social forms and institutionalisations of their interactions are important.

The third of these judgments has been a recurring theme throughout MacIntyre's publications. While MacIntyre is a Thomist he is an unusual member of this academic species in that he regards history and culture as important components of philosophical work and in particular he emphasises the importance of an 'interpreting community' in the development of intellectual traditions.

In making such an emphasis he is at one with much contemporary hermeneutical scholarship, according to which thinking always involves thinking in the context of some particular and specific public, which will normally have its own institutional structure. For example, in his seminal work *Truth and Method* Hans Georg Gadamer argued that human beings always operate from within the horizons of particular languages and traditions and thus meaning is not an objective property of the text that the interpreter discovers so much as an event in the present, a 'fusion of horizons'. In various publications MacIntyre has given examples of interpretative communities with their own institutional structures. These include: Plato's Academy, the Dominican Order of Thomas Aquinas and the different 'publics' of Gaelic highland culture and the Anglicised culture of low-land Scotland. MacIntyre argues that each of these institutional cultures embodied four principles:

1. a conception of truth beyond and ordering all truths;

2. a conception of a range of senses in the light of which utterances to be judged true or false and so placed within that ordering are to be construed;

3. a conception of a range of genres of utterance, dramatic, lyrical, historical and the like, by reference to which utterances may be classified so that we may then proceed to identify their true senses; and

4. a contrast between those uses of genres in which one way or another truth is at stake, and those governed only by standards of rhetorical effectiveness.

In MacIntyre's judgment the contemporary government funded university no longer provides such an interpretive community. Not one of the four criteria listed above characterises academic communities across disciplines and in many university departments it does not even characterise the academic communities internal to the departments. This is especially true within humanities faculties. MacIntyre believes that the fragmentation of enquiry and of understanding is taken for granted and it is presumed that each academic discipline will be autonomous and self-defining. Indeed, to assert otherwise is to suggest that there might be a 'master-narrative', some 'truth beyond and ordering all truths', to use MacIntyre's expression. Such an assertion is regarded by post-modern scholars as the greatest possible threat to intellectual freedom. This is because post-moderns at least implicitly recognise what MacIntyre takes to be foundational for a Catholic understanding of education—the idea that the ends of education can be correctly developed only with reference to the final end of human beings and the ordering of the curriculum has to be an ordering to that final end. Such a foundational principle is inimical to post-modern theories of education which begin from a stance of opposition to universals and to first and final causes. MacIntyre acknowledges the hostility of the post-modern position to the Catholic in his statement that the 'structures of the contemporary research university are deeply inimical to the project of a non-fragmented approach [to scholarship]'.

As a consequence MacIntyre believes that any Catholic university which takes seriously the proposition that Catholic education is fundamentally theological would need to have structures and goals very different from those of the great secular universities, and not just by reason of the central place given to the study of theology. Nonetheless he finds that the most prestigious Catholic universities often mimic the structures and goals of the most prestigious secular universities and do so with little sense of something having gone seriously amiss.

Moreover, MacIntyre argues that it is a shameful fact that Catholic scholars themselves contributed to the contemporary post-modern fragmentation and that one of the most significant contributors was the Spanish Jesuit Francisco Suárez (1548–1617).

Suárez fostered the 'two ends' theory of human nature by which the human being has a natural end separate from the supernatural end. Over time these two ends became equated with the secular and sacred orders, notwithstanding the fact that the notion of the *saeculum* was not initially spatialised at all—it was rather a reference to that period in history before the consummation of the world and the renewal of the cosmos. It initially referred to time, not to space. Louis Dupré in his book *Passage to Modernity* argued that the validation of an autonomous 'secular' order in late scholasticism was based on an unintentional failure to distinguish between 'pure nature' as an object of philosophical speculation, and pure nature in the order of concrete reality. In various works the twentieth-century French Jesuit Henri de Lubac noted that this failure opened the door to secularism.

With the idea of a separate natural end of the human person came the project of seeking philosophical agreement about these ends without any reference to Christian revelation. In the post-Reformation era this was seen by many to be a positive enterprise since the differences between Protestant and Catholic theologies were rendered irrelevant. However a secondary effect of this pragmatic strategy was that theology ceased to play any role in ordering the enquiries of the other disciplines. It became more and more marginalised as a discipline reserved for clerics, while the search for a common agreement about the natural ends of the person proceeded on the terrain of 'pure reason'. After a century or so of inconclusive enquiry on the plain of 'pure reason' the notion of there being any such natural end was challenged by Friedrich Nietzsche, Martin Heidegger, Jean-Paul Sartre and a whole raft of their disciples. Today we face the problem that when we try to assert a belief in a universal human nature we are told that there is no such thing and that the human species is in a state of evolutionary flux that can be improved with technological developments.

MacIntyre's critique of the self-secularisation practices of ostensibly Catholic educational institutions leads to the conclusion that new institutions need to be developed which are alert to the self-secularisation temptations, grounded in a Christocentric Trinitarian anthropology and based on the above four principles for a successful interpretative community. It is for this reason that new Catholic educational institutions are starting to mushroom in various parts of the first world which are funded by lay Catholics who do not want their children spending their late teens and early 20s writing essays for people who don't believe in truth, or objective moral goodness, let alone something as quaintly medieval as the notion of a Trinitarian God. For example, new establishments like Campion College in Sydney, the University of Notre Dame, with its campuses in Fremantle, Broome and Sydney, and Sophia University in the village of Loppiano outside of Florence, are all dedicated to the objective of offering an education that presupposes the truth of Christian revelation. Sophia University even has a Department of Trinitarian Ontology, which brings together the study of philosophy and theology in the kind of symbiotic relationship that was promoted by St John Paul II in his encyclical *Fides et Ratio*.

MacIntyre's indictment of contemporary post-Christian academies resonates with that of another prominent Scottish Catholic, Professor John Haldane from the University of St. Andrews. In an essay about how the Church needs intellectuals, Haldane lamented the fact that the new Catholic middle classes have little interest in intellectual enquiry and he blamed the Catholic education system itself for this state of affairs. He noted that instead of offering a distinctive form of education based upon a Catholic understanding of the meaning and purpose of human life, a Catholic theological anthropology in other words, Catholic tertiary institutions have sought to model their curricula on the current secular fashions in social and cultural studies. The end result is a situation wherein Catholics 'know little about the history of their faith, its distinctive content, its theological, philosophical, literary and artistic products, its traditions of spirituality', and so on.[6] Haldane suggests that some of these matters should be known about as part of Catholic cultural literacy, some for the intellectual, aesthetic and spiritual treasures they offer, and others as matters of practical religion—'truths necessary for salvation' as St Thomas would have it. Without such cultural capital there is no basis for what MacIntyre calls an interpretative community.

The Field Hospital

Pope Francis has famously said that he regards the Church as a field hospital.[7] This presupposes that the world is a battle-field. The nature of the battle we are now in has been well defined by his former Prefect for the Congregation of the Doctrine of the Faith, Cardinal Gerhard Ludwig Müller:

> Nowadays it is not uncommon to deny the existence of God or, at least, to declare with utter indifference that one is agnostically neutral. As a result, the anthropological concept that is offered to our young people puts at the centre of reality a man and a woman devoid of all transcendent meaning, reduced, as it were, to their animal instincts, making use of their freedom without any prior moral criterion. When life lacks transcendent meaning, human existence is reduced to material things, and the only reason for being or existing is pleasure, especially sexual pleasure, money, prestige or health. These are the new idols that have replaced God as man's point of reference; they have made self-sacrificing love, altruism or love of neighbour almost impossible.[8]

Pope St John Paul II said something similar back in 1987 in an address to professors at the University of Lublin. He observed that if we take away a belief in Christian revelation we usher in not only the death of God, but also the death of the human person, who, in such a materialistic universe, has no possibilities other than those offered by the material order itself. In short, if God goes, human dignity goes with him because humanity itself is reduced to the status of a commodity. And when human dignity goes, the Church needs to expand her field hospital works, patching up broken people with God's mercy and the graces which flow from the sacrament of reconciliation.

To run a field hospital however we need surgeons who understand the various pathologies, and to educate surgeons we need Catholic educational institutions that are genuinely Catholic in both form and substance, not merely in name. We need something more than anti-bullying policies and the promotion of kindness and tolerance. We need educational institutions that have as their foundation a deep understanding of a Christocentric Trinitarian anthropology with pedagogical methodologies tied to that anthropology. And we need to avoid falling into the trap of dualisms such as making sharp separations between the secular and the sacred, between religious education and so-called secular subjects, and between religious education understood as intellectual input and catechetical education understood as affective formation. Dualisms arise when things which are distinctive such as nature and grace, faith and reason, the humanity of Christ and the divinity of Christ, become separated from their intrinsic relationships to one another and treated in isolation. This is a Cartesian mode of intellectual analysis, not a Trinitarian one.

In the final analysis our educational institutions will either produce surgeons and nurses for the field hospital or victims and bodies to be patched up or buried. Because we are human we all tend to get a little bit wounded, even those of us who are the surgeons, but if we get our educational institutions right we might not merely survive the war, but actually start to rebuild a Christian civilisation.

Notes

1   A version of this chapter was presented at the Cardinal Winning Lecture, University of Glasgow, 6 February 2016.

2   V. McNabb as cited in S. Rena, *All Things Give God Glory: A Catholic Anthology* (London: Burns and Oates: 2005), p. 228.

3   G. Nebel, *Das Ereignis des Schönen* (Stuttgart: E. Klett, 1953), p. 188.

4   A. MacIntyre, *Marxism: An Interpretation* (London: SCM Press, 1953), p. 9

5   A. MacIntyre, *God, Philosophy, Universities: A Selective History of the Catholic Philosophical Tradition* (Lanham: Rowman and Littlefield, 2009).

6   J. Haldane, *The Church and the World: Essays Catholic and Contemporary* (Leominster: Gracewing, 2008) p. 125.

7   See Pope Francis, Interview in *America* magazine (30 September 2013): 'I see clearly that the thing the Church needs most today is the ability to heal wounds and to warm the hearts of the faithful; it needs nearness, proximity. I see the church as a field hospital after battle. It is useless to ask a seriously injured person if he has high cholesterol and about the level of his blood sugars! You have to heal his wounds. Then we can talk about everything else. Heal the wounds, heal the wounds ... And you have to start from the ground up."

8   G. Müller, *The Hope of the Family: A Dialogue with Gerhard Cardinal Müller* (San Francisco: Ignatius, 2014) pp. 30–33.

ON CATHOLIC EDUCATION AND INTEGRITY

Francis Campbell

T HE TITLE OF this chapter might suggest Catholic education will be presented here as a domain separate from the wider world, which counters cultural norms and considers Catholic institutions as disconnected islands in the waters of a largely non-Catholic society. This is in fact almost the exact opposite of the case to be made in what follows. Although we shall see shortly that Catholic education is certainly distinctive, we shall also see that this distinctiveness offers gifts to and for the wider world, and that these gifts are not opposed to the world beyond the Church. Rather, they will be seen to offer vital means of ensuring the *integrity* of that world. Section 1 will set the scene by examining our cultural context, and some of the discussions surrounding faith-based education in recent years. The following sections will then proceed to show the importance of Catholic education for the world outside the Church. This will involve arguing that Enlightenment secularity has strong historical and genealogical links with the traditions of Christianity, that the legacy of this tradition-rooted approach to secularity in our contemporary context is best approached through seeing our culture as pluralist, and finally that Catholic education in a pluralist context offers distinctive gifts of significant value *for* the world. This value will be seen to stem from a commitment in the Catholic educational ethos to the comprehensive formation of persons and not just professionals, and to serving the common good which can challenge the boundaries that might otherwise limit full social participation for some members of society.

In this sense we shall see a vision emerging here of Catholic education which not only fosters fruits for the wider world, but offers a safeguard on the integrity of that world. That is, the integrity of a pluralist society requires a genuine plurality of voices of differing traditions, along with widespread opportunities for full, inclusive participation. Insofar as Catholic education facilitates socialisation in these ways, then, we can approach it as a means of ensuring the integrity of contemporary society, and this standpoint should foster a confidence from Catholic educational providers in the uniqueness of their institutions and their distinctive patrimonies.[1]

Setting the Scene: Catholic Education in Contemporary Britain

Before looking at how discussions around faith-orientated education have taken shape in recent years, it is necessary to consider the climate within which these discussions have taken place, and this necessitates a definition of the word culture. Of course the task of defining culture is the subject of countless academic discussions taking place not only in cultural studies, but involving disciplines including history, philosophy, literature, anthropology and theology.[2] Owing to the enormity of this literature, let us take a widely accepted definition which mirrors the straightforward and everyday meaning of the term in its English nomenclature. T. S. Eliot famously writes that 'the word culture refers to all the characteristic activities and interests of a people',[3] and of course 'activities' here could include customs, rituals, events, and traditions, and 'interests' the beliefs or dispositional attitudes underlying those activities.

However something of the enormous complexity involved in defining culture today can be seen if we call to mind that Eliot wrote these words in 1943, when Western cultures tended to be more homogenous than today. Nowadays most of us are part of many cultural milieus, depending on the region in which we live, our race or ancestral ethnicity, our nationality, our political and ideological allegiances, and not to mention our religious faith. In this sense our 'characteristic activities and interests' tend to resemble collages or tapestries woven together by complex, intersecting histories, both individual and collective. Our domestic contemporary society, therefore, and indeed many other parts of the world (especially the West), are faced with a context of marked diversity. This presents society with a task being undertaken as never before: searching for a way to deal with ever more complex worlds of difference. Within six months of each other, both the German Chancellor, Angela Merkel, and the British Prime Minister, David Cameron, made speeches in 2013 critical of multicultural-ism, with Cameron famously saying that 'multiculturalism in Britain has failed'.[4] We need not evaluate the truth of this statement here, but to witness this sentiment being voiced at such a high-level demonstrates the point: that the ques-tion of how to navigate previously unencountered levels of cultural diversity is one of the great questions of our day.

If we broaden this discussion of culture by bringing in questions of faith, this question begins to seem even more challenging. This is so because faiths and cultures are so deeply intertwined that, as Joseph Ratzinger noted, '[in all known historical cultures, religion is the essential element …] indeed it is its determining core', as that which 'deter-mines the structure' of a culture's 'values' and 'thereby forms its inner logic'.[5] But not only are faith and cultures historically inseparable, our context today is rendered even more challenging in that faith cultures exist side-by-side with newer non-religious cultures that do not have this 'determining core'. The question of navigating deep diver-sity, then, bears particularly on the challenge of assessing what role faith plays or does not play in society. This is compounded by a growing diversity of faiths and some-times even questions about what constitutes a recognised religion and how to deal in a fair and equitable way with all faiths or beliefs and none.[6] Moreover, in this time when religious literacy is arguably more needed than ever before, the general level of religious literacy in society seems to be at an all-time low, so the faultlines between different identities can seem almost unnavigable at times.

The situation I am describing was aptly demonstrated by the soul searching that took place in the British media when David Cameron issued his Easter greetings in 2015, and sparked a lively debate by asserting that Britain was still a Christian country.[7] Strong points of view emerged on each side, with little sign of a meeting of minds as people struggled to determine or measure if the country is indeed still Christian. With many questions posed, little consensus emerged. Such discussions continue particularly around faith schools, as can be seen in the investigations into alleged attempts to influence the ethos of state schools in some parts of Birmingham in 2014, and the subsequent guidance coming from Ofsted to mitigate against this happening again.[8] As well as with occasional flashpoints like Birmingham, we have seen a debate running for many years about the role of faith schools in society and their broader contribution to British life. The core battleground of this most profound of cultural clashes is arguably the position of religious education within the state sector: that is, the position of religious communities working with financial and political mandates from a society made up of many who do not belong to those communities.

These issues and questions were demonstrated recently by the Humanist Society of Scotland, which commissioned academics in the University of St Andrews to conduct an audit of Scots Law, as they put it, 'to ascertain the nature of the intrusion of religious influence'. The audit concluded that 'education remains a sector in which the churches continued to inject considerable effort to retain a foothold in a society which is otherwise secularising rapidly'. Those who commissioned the report would probably wish to see that foothold destabilised, and to witness a removal of religion from the public sphere of the school (or university). Underlying this is the assumption that a 'de-religionised' public sphere, with no collective faith voices, is the only genuinely objective and neutral option. More specifically, this perspective would likely want to see the influence of the Church removed from the operation of educational bodies, and considerations relating to religious belief removed from the recruitment of teachers or lecturers in religious schools and universities where such considerations can function currently as an operational requirement respected in law.

The offer of a genuinely objective and neutral ('level playing field') is of course highly seductive for policymakers and politicians faced with navigating the complexity of cultural diversity described above. These policymakers may think they are grappling with unprecedented issues, but despite the prevalence of this issue in public life today, it is actually nothing new. Similar tensions gripped earlier generations as they faced the hurdle of building cohesive societies amidst a growing diversity that stretched their imaginations, causing them to think of a wider cultural canvas that could host levels of diversity that were unsettling established levels of homogeneity.

To give one example that has direct bearing on this discussion, in the nineteenth century, on the back of much Irish immigration to Britain, the Catholic Church was a faith community that stretched the prior legal norms of British society. Significant effort was invested to ensure schools were built for the most marginalised in society and that the right of parents to educate children in accordance with their consciences and without financial penalty was supported by the state. The point for this discussion is that, at least in this example, we can see that, even in nineteenth-century Britain, cultural and faith diversity was a challenge, and importantly, the precursors of today's policy makers did not shrink from that challenge by imposing a monocultural or de-religionised 'one size fits all' vision of the public sphere on its citizens.

It is easy to forget this point, and when faced with complex challenges of inclusion, simplistic and exclusivistic solutions are inevitably appealing to those in public office. For regulatory authorities it might seem easier—when faced with competing interests—to push faith out of the public sphere and impose a 'one size fits all' approach in the name of neutrality, objectivity, fairness or value for money. But these authorities are then likely to find themselves faced with even deeper questions, such as: How do we evaluate neutrality? Do secularism or humanism seem neutral to religious believers? Who defines the values of this new era, and how could a cohesive set of values be discerned to which all could subscribe? Does a 'fairness' defined by those with no faith commitment not threaten to privilege non-believers over believers? It is not only policy makers who are seduced by this allegedly neutral option, for a hostile climate can and does influence members of faith communities themselves, who retreat from the challenge of cultural complexity and artificially accommodate their own values to the dominant societal norms, undermining the distinctiveness of their identities just to blend in. But this watering down of a faith community's identity can threaten to undermine its very *raison d'être* as a distinctive way of life. Seen in this way, a supposedly objective, neutral, and de-religionised form of secularism seems highly problematic, not least as it gravely threatens to diminish our culturally rich and diverse society.

Approaching Secularism

The previous section makes clear the significant complexity of the challenge our society faces, and some of the dangers involved in denying this complexity through a particular understanding of secularism as a sphere of de-religionised neutrality. Before asking about the place of Catholic education in our world we must assess how far this form of secularism holds sway. Is our cultural context largely secularist in this way, seeing only a 'private' role for faith in the wider society? Is freedom of religious belief a mere individual freedom, deprived of the collective dimension which allows belief to manifest in society? More specifically, do we want to live in a world where the state has a monopoly on service provision in education? This would be a world where faith providers can perhaps deliver a service, but cannot call on official funds to do so. To date, faith-based education in the UK has been one of multiple numbers of service providers with the state regulating the space to sustain acceptable minimum standards in service delivery and content. In this situation, regulator and service provider must find an accommodation which respects the proper role and remit of the other. Nonetheless, there is clearly no guarantee this will always be the case: choices and priorities will always be looked at afresh, as the ongoing debates around faith schools make clear. But beneath the sometimes tedious, dry, and technical discussions taking place around this matter are deep and profound questions for society, with very far reaching consequences affecting individual roles and rights, the ability of organisations to engage and participate in public life, and even the nature of state authority and control itself.

We can thus see that weighty and penetrating discussions are required if we are to find our way through these competing views on the future of society. To look in some more detail at this, I suggest that what can be missing underneath these discussions is an appropriately accurate and nuanced understanding of the secular. In order to describe what this means, we must first examine the historical background of our current situation, and study the all-important historical context or philosophical tradition too often marginalised by the media, a marginalisation which can render these discussions oversimplified, and thus unnecessarily charged and polemical.

The historical and philosophical background is of course centred on the two centuries old rupture between faith and reason ushered into Europe at the time of the Enlightenment, and deeply rooted in different forms in European nations ever since. The interrelation of faith and reason is of course a particular concern for the Catholic tradition, where the interrelation is stated classically in *Dei Filius* with the claim that 'there can never be any real discrepancy between faith and reason'.[9] At the Second Vatican Council the consequences of this harmonious relationship for the educational sphere were drawn out: 'methodical research in all branches of knowledge, provided it is carried out in a genuinely scientific manner [...] can *never conflict* with faith'.[10] With this position as an integral aspect of Catholic thinking, it is clear that the Church's educational institutions promise to have a key role in helping to provide a space where faith and reason can constructively encounter each other. From the Catholic perspective, faith and reason are allies, and not enemies. Although at first glance this might seem like a stark piece of polemic against the Enlightenment, I want to suggest otherwise. That is, viewed from this perspective, a view of the Enlightenment—and perhaps even the secular—can emerge whereby Enlightenment reason is not an alien foe to faith commitment, but something deeply intertwined with it. In short, there might be approaches to the secular which bring this intertwining to light in effective ways. Of course this goes against the grain of many received histories of the development of European intellectualism. For much of the past two centuries the Enlightenment has been lazily classed as involving a straightforward rupture and fragmentation of faith from reason. But recent scholarship has challenged this view, as seen for example in Charles Taylor, who says that Western secularity should not be depicted as a rupture, but as an evolving story of human history with the secular and the religious dimensions not juxtaposed, but emerging from the same story.[11]

   To rectify our interpretation of the Enlightenment, Taylor suggests we need to look closely at the 'story' behind its occurrence. Among those who have attempted to do this, one key figure is Joseph Ratzinger, now Pope Emeritus Benedict XVI. Indeed, Ratzinger was one of the first to usher in what is perhaps emerging now as a new paradigm, and in this sense he can be considered a prophetic voice, a voice which challenges the seemingly outdated and oversimplified view of the Enlightenment so lacking in recent public discourse in Britain.

Ratzinger highlights a particular danger of approaching the secular as something entirely untethered from considerations of faith. This danger comes about because faith traditions are so closely linked with ethical concerns. The de-religionised secular threatens to find itself with a lacuna at its heart surrounding questions of right and wrong or good and evil. In this situation, the governing norms of the secular sphere become centered on efficacy; on human achievement and utility. It is perhaps no coincidence that the growth of new forms of technology quickly took root in European nations affected by the Enlightenment at the time of the industrial revolution. Ratzinger says there is real danger when we separate ourselves from all ethical traditions and we rely exclusively on technological reasoning and its possibilities.[12] But in raising this point he certainly does not wish to marginalise rationality. On the contrary, he sees rationality as an essential hallmark of European culture. He writes that this rationality, 'from a certain perspective, [...] has conquered the world, because the form of rationality developed first of all in Europe informs the life of every continent today. Yet this rationality can become devastating if it becomes detached from its roots and exalts technological feasibility as the sole criterion.'[13] So one issue facing the secular surrounds the sources of ethical criteria, and surely here we see a convincing example of the benefits of keeping faith and reason in conversation with each other.

Of course we are living in a time prevalent with those using religion as a vehicle for their own violent agendas. Ratzinger is fully aware of this, but he does not only acknowledge the pathologies of religion, but also the pathologies of reason.[14] He writes, 'faith in God, the idea of God, can be manipulated, and then it becomes destructive', but he claims it is also the case that a rationality which 'cuts itself off from God completely and tries to confine him to the purely subjective realm loses its bearings and thus opens the door to the forces of destruction'. He goes on, '[w]hereas the Enlightenment was searching for moral foundations that would be valid—even if God did not exist—we must invite our agnostic friends today to be open to a morality— as if God *did* exist.'[15] Perhaps ours is the optimum moment to repeat this admonition not only for reason to be policing faith, but for faith to be policing reason, and not to see faith and reason as a stark either/or choice. For Ratzinger there is a genuine complementarity here, where the searching questions of rational discourse inform the ancient traditions of faith and vice versa. He writes, '[t]here can be no peace in the world without genuine peace between reason and faith, because without peace between reason and religion, the sources of morality and law dry up.'[16]

Approaching the secular as something untethered from the religious, and the dominant narrative of rupture, leaves our culture adrift from its roots and history. Ratzinger is only one of the prophetic voices making this claim. Alasdair Macintyre raises similar concerns when he offsets Thomistic values coming up against Rousseauist ideals, and suggests that the aporia in communicating between the two could lead to a Nietzschean amorality of total chaotic relativism.[17] Doyen of the Frankfurt School, Jürgen Habermas, moves in a similar direction when he points out that, 'liberal societal structures are dependent on the solidarity of their citizens', but 'if the secularisation of society goes off the rails, the sources of this solidarity may dry up altogether'. He goes on to claim that this would 'slacken the democratic bond and exhaust the kind of solidarity that the democratic state needs, but cannot impose by law', and society disintegrates into a mere amalgamation of isolated monads acting on the basis of their own self-interest', using 'subjective rights only as weapons against each other.'[18] If solidarity is so necessary to contemporary society, then surely here we can see the value of religion, for faith-communities are—almost by definition—communities of belonging.

The secular thus needs the religious to inform ethical practice and cultivate solidarity, so let us seek to explore Taylor's claim that rather than being ruptured at the Enlightenment, we can actually see these two 'emerging from the same story.'[19] Again, Joseph Ratzinger provides a framework for this, drawing on his renowned dialogue with Habermas in the early years of the millennium. He offers us a valuable insight on the historical intertwining of faith and reason when he claims that 'secularism' is a 'fruit' of the Christian faith. By this he means that European rationality came about in countries deeply marked by centuries of Christendom specifically because Christian faith had tilled the soil with its conviction of the universality of humankind. This is seen in the political realm insofar as the Christian faith was a universal religion from the very start, and consequently could not be identified with any single state; it can be present in almost any state and can function differently in vastly different contexts. This feature of the Christian religion has tended to protect the faith from a facile over-identification with any one particular authority, so that for Christians faith is not identical to politics nor vice versa.[20] The political thus emerges as a 'secular reality with a specific role'[21] long before the Enlightenment, and it is this distinctive history which enables the great focus on that specificity to occur during the seventeenth and eighteenth centuries.

So the 'story' behind the Enlightenment can be seen as rooted in the intertwining of faith and reason at the origins of the Christian religion, and Ratzinger invites us to explore the possibilities of rediscovering that intertwining today, avoiding the rupture of one from the other, and maintaining that 'the two must be open to each other.'[22] He claims, 'only in these conditions of healthy secularity can a society be constructed in which diverse traditions, cultures and religions peacefully coexist,' and entirely to 'separate public life from all valuing of traditions, means to embark on a closed, dead-end path.'[23] We can now see that the often oversimplified and polemical tone to discussions surrounding faith-based education are lacking in the broader view expressed by Joseph Ratzinger, Alisdair MacIntyre, Jürgen Habermas and others, for whom the religious and secular are deeply historical linked, and set in a relationship of mutual complementarity.

Secularism and Pluralism in Britain

The previous section made clear that a stark contrast between reason and faith is not only inadvisable, but goes against the grain of Western history itself, including the history which gave birth to the Enlightenment. To focus now on the British context, it soon becomes apparent that the relationship between the religious and the secular differs in different contexts, and takes shape in diverse forms even within those countries touched by the Enlightenment. It came as a great shock to some, that when the former President of France made comments which directly resonate the points made above, claiming that 'secularism should not be a denial of the past' for [t]o uproot is to lose meaning; it is to weaken the foundation of national identity and to drain even more the social relationships that have such a need for memorable symbols'.[24] This was of course surprising because the French approach to the secular is very different to the British, as *laïcité* is very different to marking out a certain specificity to the secular-political realm, but rather understands the public sphere as a space which ought to be intrinsically immune from any religious influence and even expressions of faith. Gertrude Himmelfarb describes the French Enlightenment by saying that 'reason was not just pitted against religion, defined in opposition to religion; it was granted the same absolute dogmatic status as religion.'[25] We might even claim that the French Revolution was more of a belated Reformation, not fought in the name of a different interpretation of religion, but for a different form of overarching authority: a narrowly defined concept of reason. But British history is not marked in the same way by the Revolution of 1789 and the emergence of the all-powerful and domineering state based on *laïcité*.

This differentiation is seen in the fact that France (and some others) would not encourage or perhaps tolerate non-state providers or faith-based providers delivering essential services such as education on behalf of the state. That this more plural approach is found in Britain is clearly a legacy of the more careful, pragmatic and developmental way in which secular thinking took root in British society after the shockwaves were felt this side of the channel in the decades following 1789. For this reason, the public sphere was never de-religionised in Britain, and faith was thus never relegated to a privatised or domestic affair.

We have seen that Ratzinger offers us a modified approach to the secular as a 'reality with a specific role' which through constructive dialogue with faith can culti-vate 'a society be constructed in which diverse traditions, cultures and religions peacefully coexist'.[26] Through touch-ing on the British variant of the secular, we can now acknowledge that it is much closer to Ratzinger's definition than French *laïcité*. That is, the ongoing role of faith bodies in providing services like education in Britain is a product of a unique historical context and a philosophical tradition born out of that context. The historically open and inclusive approach to the active participation of faith bodies tells us much about British state and society. Moreover, a suppos-edly objective and neutral (de-religionised) approach to the secular can be seen as something quite inimical to British society, history, and culture itself.

This view of British history approaches the secular as a space in which 'diverse traditions, cultures and religions peacefully coexist', and this is exemplified by the diversity of offerings made by faith-based education providers working in consort with the state. It is thus fair to suggest that British secularity is intrinsically *pluralist*, giving room for different worldviews to work together in constructive dialogue for the good of society. There are few worldviews which have such capacities to form and transform people than religious worldviews, and few worldviews that have been transmitted across vast expanses of time and space so effectively. For this reason, how faith communities are treated can often be a litmus test for broader freedoms within the society and the place of the individual *vis-à-vis* the state. Equally, critiques by faith communities can help to reinforce democratic processes in liberal states by ensuring alternative perspectives are heard and one domineering narrative is avoided. So a faith perspective not just helps the state in terms of its efficacy through the provision of services, but actually helps to ensure the very plurality which is an integral aspect of the British tradition, at least.

In this connection, it is helpful to remind ourselves that the notion of *liberal* democracy, specifically, is meant to point to the freedoms of a genuinely liberal society, which means a freedom to challenge political authority and pose different views to the dominant norm. If secularity is not approached as intrinsically pluralist, there is a danger that these challenges will become increasingly difficult to voice, that self-proclaimed liberal democracies will become *il*-liberal and foster an unhealthy culture of uniformity. We can see Bl. John Henry Newman drawing on these aspects of liberalism in his defence of a 'liberal education' in *The Idea of a University*. There, he writes that the liberality these studies should offer, will show itself in 'a habit of mind' which 'lasts through life, of which the attributes are freedom, equitableness, calmness, moderation, and wisdom'.[27]

In short, Western democracies need the oxygen of debate and lively differences to remain vibrant, renewing, and dynamic societies. Again Habermas points us in that direction, highlighting how attentive the state must be to preserving plurality, claiming 'it is in the interest of the constitutional state to deal carefully with all the cultural sources that nourish its citizens' consciousness of norms and their solidarity.'[28]

The pluralism I am presenting here must be approached not only as 'horizontal' and sensitive simply to the different voices on offer at any moment in history. It also needs to be open to the 'vertical' dimension of time, to the distinct historical and philosophical context which gave it birth. This calls for an inclusivity which is attentive to the Christian roots of British society, which are reflected across a whole set of norms from the legal to the parliamentary. Calling to mind Ratzinger's comments about 'healthy secularity', there are good grounds to state that it is British society's Judaeo-Christian foundations which provide the pluralist platform on which others can integrate, engage and participate. British state governance has offered a working system which has managed over the centuries to include and integrate various differences of faith. In my view it is preferable to draw on this organically developed tradition than to try and impose an alien version of absolutist secularism from outside. Such an approach in the UK context would create unnecessary ruptures in society and perhaps usher in further marginalisation of specific groups who would be denied the right of collective engagement and participation.

The integral heart of pluralism is the openness which allows for a variety of voices rather than a monotone, officially authorised, narrative. A plural space will often be open to greater participation by religious groups and other organisations and avoid authoritarian tendencies. A truly pluralist society will often be characterized by a weaker state often acting as a regulator, but open to a variety of providers meeting acceptable standards and contributing to the flourishing of wider society. Pluralism is thus the space allowing the coexistence in civic peace of different racial, ethnic and religious groups, with active social interaction between them. Pluralism is not just the toleration of difference, but constructive exchange with, and interest in, the other. Pluralism should not merely allow but encourage different groups to participate and engage in society through collective organizations. In the following section we shall see that this view of pluralism means that, not only are the different voices at work in a pluralist society safeguarding and preserving genuine plurality itself, but that to do so they must equally safeguard and preserve their own distinctiveness.

Catholic Education and Integrity

I can now bring this chapter to a close by making the final point as outlined at the beginning: that the distinctive gifts of Catholic education not only enrich the Catholic community, but offer a vital means to ensure the integrity of the society outside the Church. To make this point, we need first to look at examples of these distinctive gifts, and two which promise to serve particularly well here are firstly a person-centred approach to education, and secondly an educational ethos centred on a concern for the common good of society.

Person-centred Educators

The distinctively Catholic—or perhaps even indeed Christian—approach to education can be summed-up with the desire to expand each person's capacity for love. On the most basic level, love is held by Catholic tradition as the most fundamental desire of the human being; a fundamental 'passion' which is 'aroused by the attraction of the good'.[29] All people are thus considered to be directed fundamentally by love, by a desire to achieve the good. Viewed theologically, love is the fullest expression of the human being in the sight of God, the 'theological virtue by which we love God above all things for his own sake, and our neighbour as ourselves'.[30] In this way love functions for the Catholic tradition as a kind of source and summit of human identity, and therefore the expansion of the capacity to love in Catholic education should take shape as the cultivation of a person's humanity, or better, their full human personhood. This in turns means that Catholic education is intrinsically holistic, fostering all the dimensions of their personhood: body, mind and spirit. In this connection, the deep relationship between Catholic education and integrity is shown to be fundamental: for the word integrity is derived from the Latin *integer*, meaning 'whole', and Catholic education is by definition concerned with the whole person.

When Pope Benedict XVI spoke at St Mary's University Twickenham, in September 2010, he called on Catholic schools never to lose sight of the immensely important task of forming persons. He reminded us that Catholic education is not a matter of ensuring the efficacy (as earners or workers) of individual people, of seeking to equip students with professional skills and academic competences. Rather, he said that all these tasks must be ordered to the fundamental context of growing in friendship with God, and interrelated with the inestimable gifts and fruits which flow from that friendship. In this sense, Catholic schools were reminded not just to focus on making good students, but good citizens, and most fundamentally, good persons.

On that day Pope Benedict echoed the sentiment of John Henry Newman's *Idea*, which calls for universities to be places where a thousand schools make contributions and where the academic formation is wide and inter-woven across disciplines. In Newman's words, university education gives people 'a clear, conscious view of their own opinions and judgments, a truth in developing them, an eloquence in expressing them, and a force in urging them.'[31] This is the distinctive offer of a Catholic and Christian education. This is a form of education which calls us to remember the bigger picture, to think about formation in its widest sense so that it is not simply about acquiring a trade or a profession, although these are of course important and taken seriously in their own right. The distinctive offer of Catholic education is about living a fulfilled life and forming persons, meaning individual subjects in whom virtue is fostered, who can make sound judgements, and grow into the fullness of their character. Retaining this grand horizon in an era of ever-increasing specialisation in education and with faculties often retreating into sub-subject silos can be challenging. Newman's idea of authentic education is that the learning takes place in inter-disciplinary encounters; broadening the horizons of the mind and therefore forming character. This does not entail a diminishing in the value of the vocational dimension, but rather seeks to ensure that this dimension is always balanced with a comprehensive academic formation which equips the student in the broadest possible sense.

The Common Good Ethos

The Catholic Church has been following the approach being described here for a considerable period of time, affecting the development and formation of countless persons. Each day the Catholic Church alone is educating nearly sixty million students globally through its institutions. Nonetheless Catholic education is not without its critics, as we have seen. Some deny their very right to exist, and especially to enjoy state subsidy or subvention. There are practical objections too. Some claim that denominational schooling fosters division, mistrust and even hatred. The evidence on Catholic schooling suggests otherwise. Not only is there no body of evidence which shows that graduates of denominational schooling are more prone to negative behaviour, but the recent report by Duncan Morrow on Scotland's Catholic schools showed that they simply did not cause sectarianism.[32] Across many Catholic (and Anglican) schools it is noticeable that they have significant numbers of students coming from other faith communities, who are actually attracted to the distinctive gifts of a Christian schooling. In the very different context of Pakistan, I myself have witnessed the same pattern, seeing many Christian schools with a majority of Muslim students.

Critics of denominational schooling would also have us believe that faith schools are not representative of wider society and tend to serve privilege. Again, the evidence seems to suggest otherwise. Catholic schools in England have just over 70% of students coming from a Catholic back-ground and 55% of the teaching staff. The most recent statistics show that not only are Catholic schools more ethnically diverse than the national average, but they also take more students from deprived areas, and so are bastions of an economic diversity at a time when society seems to be moving in the other direction. Moreover, the evidence shows that this diversity does not come at the expense of quality. Catholic schools have a higher number of Ofsted ranked good or outstanding than non-Catholic schools, and students score higher in GCSEs and SATs than the national average.[33]

The statistics just given make it clear that Catholic education can stand alongside non-religious education and withstand the criticisms of privilege, exclusivism, or low academic standards. In this sense (and according to nar-rowly defined secular norms), the Church is a highly effective provider of education amongst the plurality on offer in contemporary society. But let us not forget Pope Benedict's reminder that the identity of a Catholic school or university is not simply about numbers or course content, but about conviction. The constant integration of the ethos with the educational philosophy reminds all concerned of the broader goals of Catholic education. In this sense, the inclusivity and diversity of Catholic schools, and their impressive results, should not be seen as validating their existence according to narrow secular norms of efficacy, but as the flowering of the deep-rooted Catholic concern for the common good of society. Therefore, educating non-Catho-lics, educating students from diverse ethnic backgrounds, educating those from challenging economic circumstanc-es—and doing all this successfully—is not an attempt to accommodate Catholic education to society, but part of the very ethos of the Catholic tradition. Moreover, we see here once again how closely linked Catholic education is with integrity, remembering the root-word *integer* in relation to this clear concern for the good of the *whole* society.

In this connection it is worthwhile sounding a note of caution to ensure educators do not lose sight of the broader vision of the Catholic ethos described by Pope Benedict in September 2010. Retaining integration with the secular requires constant attention. Getting the balance right all the time will not always be easy, especially with pressures from within a professional educational culture that understandably demands ever more inputs and data to be able to measure impact and value for money. But the Catholic school or university needs to be as attentive to its ethos and identity as it is to the essential professional metrics, and the argument made here would suggest that the two can cohere quite comfortably, or to repeat the words of *Gaudium et Spes* again, 'methodical research' if carried out genuinely and rationally, 'can *never conflict* with faith'.[34]

In conclusion, this chapter argues that it is more appropriate to speak of culture as pluralist rather than simply secular. Pluralism is more organic to our experience in these islands over recent centuries than secularism. Second, that in such a pluralist world, faith and people of faith can have a place and contribute through individual and collective action to the goals of wider society. And third, that faith based educational institutions have a distinctive offering in such a pluralist world provided they retain a commitment to a clear identity which distinguishes their approach and is complementary to other providers in the educational space. Our opportunity is to create a vibrant space where faith and reason are not pitted against each other, but are respectful of each other and help to provide a meaningful platform for intellectual engagement rather than disengagement which is occurring in many parts of our world.

Of course this vision will prove challenging along the way. But engagement and participation is always preferable to isolation and marginalisation both for state and Church. Pluralism has given us a wonderful faith-based education system which allows us to live up to Newman's challenge. We have a system that has evolved and depends on a delicate equilibrium which must be promoted, explained, and if need be defended, in the political and public arena. This reality is not without its tensions and challenges, but it remains a fine example of a mutually beneficial relationship within a pluralist society between state and faith which works to the benefit of both, but most of all for the citizens of this society. It has the potential to answer a much needed response to our contemporary culture as we struggle to define and build cohesive communities. It has worked for previous generations and is our story. We must be beacons of hope in promoting the social values of a shared community: compassion, justice, awareness of the needs of others—especially the poorest in our society. In summary, the distinctive integrity of Catholic education promises to foster the integrity of our pluralist world, through its cultivation of the integrity of persons and all members of society.

Notes

1   I am undertaking this discussion as someone who is tasked with navigating a Catholic University which is also a public university, namely St Mary's University Twickenham, and so this chapter tries to straddle the world of theory and practice.

2   For good discussions on the complexity of the task of defining culture see R. Williams, *Keywords: A Vocabulary of Culture and Society* (Oxford: Oxford University Press, 1985), or from a theological perspective, T. Rowland, *Culture and the Thomist Tradition: After Vatican II* (Abingdon: Routledge, 2003) and T. Gorringe, *Furthering Humanity: A Theology of Culture* (Abingdon: Routledge, 2004.)

3   T. S. Eliot, *Notes Toward a Definition of Culture* (London: Faber & Faber, 1962), p. 14

4   D. Cameron, 'Speech on radicalisation and Islamic extremism', Munich, 5 February 2011, in *New Statesman*, http://www.newstatesman.com/blogs/the-staggers/2011/02/terrorism-islam-ideology.

5   J. Ratzinger, 'Christ, Faith and the Challenge of Cultures.' Speech given in Hong Kong to the presidents of the Asian Bishops' Conferences in March 1993, as found at http://www.ewtn.com/library/CURIA/RATZHONG.HTM

6   For a discussion of a high-profile case surrounding the definition of Scientology, see B. Tonking, 'The Scientology case is about freedom: now how about Jedi?' in *The Independent*, 13 December 2013.

7   P. Prince, 'David Cameron declares: "Britain is still a Christian country"', in *Daily Telegraph*, 5 April 2015.

8   See the full Ofsted report on 'Operation Trojan Horse': 'Report into allegations concerning Birmingham schools arising from the 'Trojan Horse' letter' at https://www.gov.uk/government/uploads/system/uploads/attachment_dat a/file/340526/HC_576_accessible_-.pdf

9   Vatican I, *Dei Filius* 4.

10 Vatican II, *Gaudium et spes* 36 (my emphasis). Note the word scientific (*scientiarum*) here means something closer to the word 'academic' or the German *wissenschaftlich* than the English 'scientific', that is, not just disciplines of natural science like biology, physics and chemistry but academic disciplines in the broadest sense.

11 C. A. Taylor, *A Secular Age* (Cambridge, MA: Belknap Press of Harvard University, 2007.)

12 J. Ratzinger, *Europe Today and Tomorrow: Addressing the Fundamental Issues* (San Francisco: Ignatius Press, 2007), p 42

13 *Ibid.*, p 43

14 *Ibid.*, p. 93

15 *Ibid.*, p. 96 (my emphasis)

16 *Ibid.*, p. 93

17 A. McIntyre, *After Virtue* (London: Bloomsbury Academic, 2007), especially pp. 109–120.

18 J. Habermas in J. Habermas and J. Ratzinger, *Dialectics of Secularisation: On Reason and Religion* (San Francisco: Ignatius Press, 2006), p. 35.

19 See Taylor, *A Secular Age*.

20 This sentiment was recently echoed by Pope Francis who said in an interview with French periodical La Croix that 'States must be secular. Confessional states end badly.' http://www.la-croix.com/Religion/Pape/INTERVIEW-Pope-Francis-2016-05-17-1200760633

21 Pope Benedict XVI, *Interview on journey to France*, 12 September 2008.

22 *Ibid.*

23 Pope Benedict XVI, *Message to new Ambassador to San Marino*, 13 November, 2008.

24 See N. Sarkozy, 'Address on the relations between Church and the State', Hall of Conciliation at St John Lateran, 20 December 2007, as cited in J. R. Allen, 'Extracts from Sarkozy on church/state relations in France' in *National Catholic Reporter*, 10 September 2008.

25 G. Himmerfarb, *The Roads to Modernity* (New York: First Vintage Books, 2005), p. 152.

26 Pope Benedict XVI, *Interview on journey to France*, 12 September 2008.

27 J. H. Newman, *The Idea of a University* (New Haven & London: Yale University Press, 1996), p. 77.

28 Habermas, *Dialectics of Secularization*, p. 46
29 *Catechism of the Catholic Church*, §1765.
30 *Ibid.*, §1822.
31 Newman, *The Idea of a University*, p. 127.
32 See http://www.sconews.co.uk/latest-edition/45509/sectarianism-report-catholic-schools-not-to-blame-for-problem/
33 See the statistical data of the Catholic Education Service website for exact figures: http://www.catholiceducation.org.uk/ces-census
34 Vatican II, *Gaudium et spes*, 36.

THE CATHOLIC INTELLECTUAL

Raymond McCluskey

DECADES BEFORE THE distinguished Illinoisan prelate-scholar, Rev. John Tracy Ellis, published in 1955 his influential and oft-discussed article on 'American Catholics and the Intellectual Life', another man-of-letters had already drawn close attention to the perceived lack of intellectuals in the American Catholic community. The author of this earlier piece, Dr Thomas O'Hagan, was, in fact, Canadian but he cast his eye across the entire North American continent:

> There is perhaps nothing that our Catholic people in America need more today than a great intellectual awakening. . . Are Catholic young men and women reaching out intellectually into the world around them? Is it not true that in many quarters there is intellectual stagnation among Catholics?[1]

In seeking to provide a rationale for Catholics' apparent unwillingness to engage in intellectual pursuit, O'Hagan did not hold back in pointing the finger of blame: 'I am inclined to believe that a part of this vanity and frivolousness is cultivated in our schools. Even they sometimes are not free from the dangerous microbes of fads.'[2] There would appear to be nothing new under the sun in terms of scapegoating schools for failing to deal with all manner of social ills. Yet the accusation of O'Hagan in 1916 was presented in more nuanced fashion by Ellis almost 40 years later when he famously suggested that there had been an 'overemphasis which some authorities of the Church's educational system in the United States have given to the school as an agency for moral development, with an insufficient stress on the role of the school as an instrument for fostering intellectual excellence'.[3]

Ellis' analysis of his perceived dearth of Catholic intellectual activity and excellence in the United States was, in fact, touching on a raw contemporary nerve which manifested itself in re-printings throughout the world. In the UK, *The Tablet* serialised the original article over three weeks at the end of 1956.[4] Nevertheless, in the English-speaking world since Ellis, it has primarily been American scholarship which has picked up the baton and taken a lead in exploring the nature and role of the Catholic intellectual. It is that scholarship—with some non-US exceptions—which must constitute the foundations for the present chapter.

The Intellectual

It is probably true to record here, based on anecdotal evidence alone, that to describe oneself as 'an intellectual' in the English-speaking world is to be greeted with at best passive disinterest and at worst active distrust. The intellectual needs to get 'a real job'. In France, on the other hand, the words 'je suis intellectuel' are a badge of honour with, for some, accompanying celebrity status.[5] Of course, this is an over-simplistic distinction. Nonetheless, for those who live their lives in the environs of universities or other institutions of higher learning in the USA, Canada, Australia, New Zealand, Ireland or the UK, it is sometimes hard to grasp that large numbers of the broader populations may not consider them as in touch with 'the real world'.[6]

For the purposes of this chapter, what is 'an intellectual'? One would think that definition could be straightforward: something along the lines of 'a custodian and generator of ideas'. But, as ever, definitions only lead to new questions, demanding new emphases. Steve Fuller, in a rigorous discussion, has emphasised that 'intellectual' and 'academic' are not necessarily synonymous and, indeed, other scholars such as James T. Fisher have advocated recognition of the intellectual vitality of, for example, journalists and artists working in the TV and motion picture media.[7] Fuller's presence in the discourse is a timely reminder that a great deal of what has been written in recent years about the nature of 'the intellectual' is driven by sociological enquiry about the nature of intellectuals' contribution to any given society and, even more fundamentally, the manner in which intellectuals think of themselves or, to put it another way, self-identify. In their seminal survey of intellectuals, Charles Kurzman and Lynn Owens delineated three major paradigms with regard to how intellectuals understood themselves and their role: as a class-in-themselves; as primarily class-bound (often acting as mediators for related ideologies); as relatively class-less, able to transcend their group of origin to pursue independent ideals.[8] In addressing the role of the Catholic intellectual, such contributions from the wider academy must not be ignored.

The Catholic Intellectual

It is, however, important that in considering the role of the Catholic intellectual, a positive frame-of-mind be established from the outset. The challenge facing the promoter of Catholic intellectual life has been succinctly summarised by Marcia Colish: the argument that 'if one is a Catholic, one has to cash in one's brains'.[9] Yet, the response to such a perception cannot be apologetical defensiveness. As any serious student of theology or history will be able to substantiate, the study of the inherited legacy of the Christian past is not without its difficulties. This is precisely because the Christian is not allowed to turn one's brain off for fideism—at its most extreme, a negation of human reason in seeking knowledge of the divine—has never been the orthodox Christian way.[10] The Catholic faith involves elements of struggle, a constant search for concordance between 'fides' and 'ratio', faith and reason.

The clue to a Catholic usage of 'the intellectual' begins with the etymology of the word itself. The Latin *intellectum* in the Middle Ages denoted 'understanding', a deep, transformative grasp of a person(s) or thing(s). The biblical roots are scattered throughout the Old and New Testaments, most notably in the Vulgate translation of the Book of Psalms, where Psalm 110 refers, for example, to 'understanding' achieved through the practice of keeping the commandments and Psalm 118 makes the claim that the psalmist has more 'understanding' than all his teachers.[11] Throughout subsequent centuries, by way of the likes of Augustine of Hippo (354–430), Anselm of Canterbury (1033–1109), Teresa of Ávila (1515–82), and Cardinal John Henry Newman (1801–90), the goal of better understanding the divine and the nature of God's relationship with human beings has been a constant impetus to intellectual and spiritual endeavour. Anselm's famous dictum—*credo ut intelligam* (I believe in order to understand)—remains a source of philosophical enquiry in seeking to grasp more fully the way in which faith can, indeed, illuminate one's grasp of reality.[12] Yet Anselm was both monk and archbishop; he, as in the case of many generations of Christian thinkers, would not have identified himself as 'an intellectual', as a person who, to put it bluntly, *inhabits* or *does* understanding.

As Lewis Perry has pointed out, the application of the label 'intellectual' to a person, certainly in the English-speaking world, is an early twentieth-century invention.[13] Nevertheless, there continued to be Catholic scholars throughout the Enlightenment period, contrary to any narrative which would seek to distance Catholicism more generally from innovative currents in the sciences and humanities, except for occasions of condemnation and disavowal.[14] With the onset of the twentieth century, claims have been made, both in the US and the UK, that there was a veritable *renaissance* in Catholic intellectual endeavours, with a new sense of purpose particularly in the years between the two World Wars.[15] Finally, in the period since the Second Vatican Council (1962–65) and onwards into the present age, there has been, perhaps, a greater sense of Kurzman and Owens' second paradigm but understood as not so much bound by class as linked to perceived 'liberal' or 'conservative' mindsets. The modern descendant of the epistolary tradition of past centuries is the online blog in which much intellectual energy is expended, for good or ill.[16]

Of course, countless studies of the intellectual history of the ancient, medieval and modern worlds have drawn attention to the complex ebb-and-flow of ideas—of thesis and counter-thesis—across the centuries.[17] In 1972, Thomas O'Dea sought to present a magisterial synthesis of the Catholic intellectual's particular contribution since the Tridentine era of the 16th century.[18] With the closure of the Second Vatican Council only seven years previous, with Paul VI still on the chair of Peter, and with (most importantly in terms of balancing hindsight) the papacies of John Paul II and Benedict XVI still in the future, it is extremely interesting to review O'Dea's perspectives on the past, present and future of 'the Catholic intellectual'. Perhaps a key observation, certainly worthy of critical attention, is O'Dea's assertion that the modern Catholic intellectual ideally rejects the *ahistoricism* of the past, 'making the sense of history and its implications their own'.[19] In a way, O'Dea seems to be applauding a new-found speaking directly to the issues of the day rather than indulgent rehearsal of arcane arguments. In doing so, he is quite optimistic about the future role of the Catholic intellectual. However, he also noted, in light of remarks by the eminent philosopher Jacques Maritain (1882–1973), the spread of a 'kind of anarchy' amongst intellectuals. The end-result could be one of two things: either a more flexible and creative Catholicism or a Church in the process of 'self-liquidation'.[20]

Anyone familiar with the contemporary novel *Catholics* by Brian Moore (1921–99) will immediately recognise that O'Dea was not alone in this period in foretelling the possibility of a Church as a social movement without transcendental pretensions.[21] O'Dea's particular insight lies in his pointing out the particular responsibilities of Catholic intellectuals in meeting the difficult challenges ahead. In fact, the immediate post-Conciliar decade saw the emergence of a range of 'renewal' movements in the English-speaking world, some more long-lasting than others, which metaphorically created a cacophony of discourse and discussion. The Scottish experience here was not untypical with clerical, religious and lay participation in reading groups and public lectures designed to facilitate explorations of 'new' theological thinking emerging at the time.[22] However, the challenge for the likes of the Newman Association, founded originally in the UK in 1942 as a forum for Catholic graduates' continuing intellectual development in faith-related issues, has always been one of attracting more recruits beyond the core circles of active, enthusiastic members. Even at an anecdotal level, one begins to wonder if there is, indeed, a persistent streak of 'anti-intellectualism' present in contemporary Catholicism. In short, must the writer on the Catholic *intellectual* also address the phenomenon of the Catholic *anti*-intellectual?

In fact, an empirical study in 1993 led the way on this very question in the US context. Daniel Rigney and Thomas Hoffman put under the microscope the hypothesis that Catholicism in America inhabited an 'anti-intellectual religious culture'.[23] They used a variety of 'barometers', including tolerance of pluralistic discourse, newspaper reading and literary and professional memberships.[24] Significantly, their findings were mixed. While there was no hard evidence that Catholics were different from others in terms of a 'broad spectrum' of relevant criteria, there were, on certain key indicators, some relatively disappointing indicators in terms of what might be termed consistent intellectual curiosity and engagement.[25] However, the two authors ended their study on an optimistic note, grounded in 'impressive educational strides' which, ultimately, provided reason for optimism for the future of Catholic intellectual life in the US.[26]

Rigney and Hoffman's sanguinity was based on a reading of the work of the American priest-sociologist, Andrew Greeley (1928–2013). In truth, Greeley's treatments of Catholic education in his contemporary America were far from one-dimensional—he was certainly ready to offer unflinching critique—but he did underline the social capital which the Catholic school transmitted from generation to generation.[27] Such an understanding really takes its cue from the work of James Coleman for whom social capital exists in the *'relations* among persons.'[28] One can readily see how such an insight might be relevant in an analysis of the interplay between teachers and students in schools, colleges and universities. In its most idealistic sense, theirs is a symbiotic relationship for who can be a teacher without a student to teach? What is the student without a teacher from whom to learn? It is a circle of inter-dependence constant in its demands and expectations. Social capital accrues through the incremental sharing of teachers and students in the mission, values, and sectorial reputation of Catholic schools and colleges.[29] The impact of such seminal experiences should, ultimately, be felt in wider society through the contributions of citizens formed through Catholic education.[30]

However, it is at this point that a troubling question must be posited—troubling in the sense of needing to be asked but difficult in the answering. Does Catholic education as part of its *defining identity* vigorously seek to encourage intellectual curiosity and, ultimately, the formation of minds passionate about engaging with the world through the cultivation of the aesthetic senses and the articulation, exchange and reception of ideas? To be clear: this is not a question which requires a response citing numbers of Catholic graduates in the humanities or which expects an answer in which judgement is passed concerning, for example, the competing prioritisation of playing for the college football team or pursuing research in the university library.[31] This would be to put the cart before the horse. A reply to the question really requires an examination of what Catholic education is supposed to be about *in the first place.* Is the formation of 'intellectuals' even a goal of Catholic education in the twenty-first century? If not, should it be?

Nurturing 'the Intellectual' in Catholic Education

First, a Catholic response needs to take cognisance of the broader scholarly discourse surrounding 'the intellectual' (as has already been emphasised above). This includes study of the contributions of those who are not Catholic but have challenging things to say which can generate new and revealing insights. Antonio Gramsci (1892–1937), for example, saw the issue of the role of intellectuals essentially in *cultural* terms, calling for the *organic* emergence of a new class of intellectuals, transforming the inherited power structures of society.[32] Henry Giroux, the distinguished educational theorist, has more recently looked to teachers to usher students into a culture of 'critique, possibility and democracy'.[33] At root, one detects an image of the intellectual as a challenger of the status quo and advocacy of the teacher *as intellectual* must necessarily enshrine a desire to effect transformation. This is entirely in tune with the aspirations of Catholic education. This is not to say, of course, that writers such as Gramsci and Giroux can be superficially enlisted as props for the mission of Catholic education. This would be an unsophisticated treatment. But Catholic teachers *do* need to reflect on the ways in which they are called to transform lives through their words and actions: in other words, through their conscientious professionalism. There is much in the world which may require serious challenge. Encouragement amongst students to maintain critical distance in discussion is important. As the *Congregation for Catholic Education* stated in an *instrumentum laboris* in 2014:

> [There] are reflective skills, for instance, by which we are responsible for our actions, or intercultural, decision-making, citizenship skills, that are becoming increasingly important in our globalised world and affect us directly, as is the case with skills related to consciousness, critical thinking and creative and transforming action.[34]

The language of the Congregation here is ostensibly about 'skills' rather than 'ideas'. Yet sensitivity to global issues, criticality in debate, and creativity in confronting pressing social issues must surely be predicated on a (albeit sometimes quite basic) philosophical grasp of related concepts and vocabulary which allows students to articulate their concerns and intended actions. In fact, the word 'intellectual' appears only once in the Congregation's document and, in that instance, it features as an adjective rather than as a noun: teaching is presented as guidance towards taking 'important intellectual, social and political responsibilities in local communities'.[35] The link between 'intellectual' and 'responsibilities' is what is so telling here. Actions of Catholic social justice are born out of an intellectual grasp of what is the right thing to do. This insight must surely resonate with any committed Catholic educator. Indeed, the mandate to 'change the world' is nothing less than biblical in inspiration. As such, one would have thought that every Catholic is called to be 'intellectual' in a sense which encourages both the reflective and the active.

Second, Catholic schools should seek to nurture the intellectually joyful, as well as curious, individual.[36] Michael Kirwan has recently drawn attention to historical trends in Jesuit thought which emphasised 'existential purpose' (praise, reverence and service of God) and 'participative delight' (joy in the presence of God) in relation to the *Spiritual Exercises* of St Ignatius of Loyola.[37] This is a timely insight, reminding the reader that Catholic intellectual life should be driven by a curiosity which is rooted not just in 'delight' but, above all, 'love', reflecting the very being of God. Indeed, the roots of this understanding stretch much further back than the sixteenth century.[38] Monastic 'love of learning' has been cogently portrayed as having promoted networks of learning in the early and central Middle Ages which created the conditions for the emergence of urban universities (Paris, Bologna, Oxford) and the schools of later centuries which, ultimately, left their

progenitors behind as societies' needs and contours
changed.[39] Be that as it may, the 'love of learning' characteristic of medieval Benedictine communities and others is
there to be imitated once more, particularly in an online
world which would seem to have echoes of those monastic
networks of centuries ago, sustained as they were by a
veritable industry of letter-writing, manuscript loans and
personal visitations. There is nothing to patronise here in
seeking inspiration for the Catholic educator of the present
day. Just as Mike Higton has so eloquently sought to
challenge the distorted narrative which would have one
believe that the medieval University of Paris only gained
in rational insight as its religious adhesions diluted—a
paradigm designed to fit in with an understanding of steady
onwards progress of intellectual endeavour towards the
crystal-clear vistas of modernity—so too the monasteries of
medieval Europe offer exempla of an intellectual curiosity
drawn from deep wells of spiritual contemplation and
patristic wisdom.[40] In sum, the Catholic intellectual should
not be afraid to draw from across the centuries of insight
available to him or her. The sense of a long established
intellectual tradition is strong. It is a matter of determina-
tion and will to bring students in Catholic education of the
modern day into a thoughtful encounter with this tradition.[41]

Third, the Catholic intellectual should be robust in
dialogue with others with whom there may be disagree-
ments, but ever resistant to the mere cleverness of wit and
soundbite or the purveying of a sense of any kind of
superiority. The medium of communication is important in
this. The online pithy comment recorded within the stric-
tures of a certain number of characters is certainly not to be
rejected out-of-hand like some latter-day Luddite but it is
surely no elitist conceit to ask that there be greater awareness of the limits of the genre. The briefest phrase, of course,
can lock in a wealth of thought and insight. One need only
think of the Japanese haiku tradition or the collected *pensées*
of the French moralists François-René de Chateaubriand

(1768–1848) or Joseph Joubert (1754–1824).[42] But, as James Schall has argued, intellectual questions 'are not just questions' but are 'intended to have answers'.[43] The Catholic intellectual, consequently, should aim to provide answers to issues of import in the world which, while faithful to one's own principles forged through considered reflection on the teaching and intellectual tradition of the Church, nevertheless model the sort of patience and irenic spirit which is necessary for social cohesion in a pluralist present. Ideally, the traditional essay, article (journal or newspaper), or monograph (particularly for Catholic academics in the humanities) remain the bread-and-butter of such discourses, while there is little doubt that the (no longer so) new media are making inroads into those conventional carriers of existential debate. Catholic intellectuals have been here before, taking on the 'clothes' of neo-Scholasticism in the nineteenth century, for example, to provide 'for the defence and beauty of the Catholic faith'.[44]

What Pope Francis has made clear is that the task ahead in the twenty-first century is not one of defence but of invitation.[45] The Catholic intellectual must rise to that challenge, finding a language which conveys the attraction of faith to a world which oftentimes seems unwilling to listen. Partaking of this task will require the fresh intellectual energies of generations to come. It will be necessary for Catholic schools, colleges and universities to work hard on raising the status of a whole range of disciplines, making the study of, for example, the humanities and sciences so inviting and stimulating as to challenge the status of professions such as medicine and law. Not least, there needs to be real, spirited advocacy of the vocation of the Catholic teacher in schools. However, the horse may already have bolted on this issue of perceived status of career choices. If that is, indeed, the case, there would seem to be a long road yet to travel before Pope Francis's vision of the Church can be fully realised on the ground.[46]

Finally, there needs to be a more cultivated appreciation in Catholic education regarding the power of the arts as a vehicle for positive impact on people's lives. Catholic artists, musicians, writers, actors, while not necessarily academics, remain 'intellectuals' in terms of their involvement in the generation of ideas and their inhabiting of spaces where public impact is effected. While it does need to be acknowledged that the presentation of the arts as a means of 'social uplift' has certainly occasioned reservations amongst some commentators since the 1990s at least, nevertheless there would seem to be firm ground in arguing that the arts offer the *possibility* of speaking to the hearts and minds of listeners and observers beyond the confines of the Academy.[47] For example, there is powerful testimony relating to the impact of the arts as stimulators of religious vitality and social transformation.[48] Sir James MacMillan (b. 1959) points to music's ability to reveal what 'lurks in the crevices of the human-divine experience'.[49] Una Cadegan references the Catholic novelist Walter Percy (1916–90) in launching a reflection on the vicissitudes of Catholic intellectual life in modern times.[50] James Fisher and Margaret McGuinness propose that the promotion of the artistic imagination has led to an 'ongoing construction of a Catholic intellectual tradition' which has evidenced an ability to incorporate 'physical and aesthetic elements that had otherwise been cast aside as anti-intellectual.'[51] Such witnesses, as it were, may at first sight appear disparate, even random, in their selection but, in fact, they are univocal in their assertion that the arts have provided—and can provide again—a meeting point for profound ideas of spirituality and transcendence communicated through a whole range of multifarious outputs. A new confidence needs to be generated amongst Catholic artists, beginning in the schools and nurtured further in higher education wherever possible, in proactively seeking out opportunities for using their talents in responding to one of the great challenges of the modern age: speaking 'heart to heart' and 'mind to mind' in a conversation between Christian faith and the secular world. Indeed, this is not only a task for Catholics. The Distinguished Professor of Humanities at Baylor University, Alan Jacobs, has recently urged that Christian intellectuals re-discover their role as the 'bridger of cultural gaps', talking less to one another and more to the culture around them.[52] Catholics in the arts have a real contribution to make to that urgent agenda of outreach and continuing dialogue, grounded in charity and hope.

Concluding Remarks

The principal aim of this chapter has been to re-focus attention on the person of the Catholic intellectual. It has sought to alert the reader to the deep seams of scholarly discourse relating to the place and role of the intellectual within the faith community and in wider society more generally. For the Dominican scholar Antonin-Gilbert Sertillanges (1863–1948), the intellectual vocation was only for the few, such were the privations to be faced in the search for profundity of utterance; indeed, Sertillanges proposed an entirely regimented way of life for the scholar.[53] Today, in the second decade of the twenty-first century, the figure of the Catholic intellectual, male and female, is much more fluid, crossing the boundaries of academe into the arts, media and sciences. One task which continues to focus minds is seeking clearer links between the Catholic intellectual tradition and the range of disciplines which students will encounter.[54] The key, however, must be to encourage a love of ideas in whatever context, modelling for young people especially a desire to be challenged and not to accept uncritically the latest cultural preferences.[55] While this chapter makes no claim to comprehensiveness of treatment of its theme, there can be no ambiguity about what is its principal message: that the formation of intellectual interests and aspirations amongst students requires an educational environment in which active and critical engagement with ideas is consistently awarded high value in terms of social and cultural capital. Intellectual curiosity, a passion for knowledge and understanding, and a deep desire to engage in irenic discourse with the modern world: these aspirations need to be clearly articulated for the benefit of all, not just any perceived elitist few. They should be a *sine qua non* in Catholic education. Such aspirations are now imperatives as the Church seeks to continue its mission not only in the face of the existential challenges of today but also in responding to those which the future will undoubtedly bring.

Notes

1   T. O'Hagan, *Essays on Catholic Life* (Baltimore: John Murphy Company, 1916), pp. 135, 140. On O'Hagan, see J. T. Hurley, 'Thomas O'Hagan, Pioneer Poet and Scholar' in *Canadian Catholic Historical Association Report* vol. 17 (1955), pp 79–87. Forty years after the publication of O'Hagan's volume would appear J. T. Ellis, 'American Catholics and the Intellectual Life' in *Thought* vol. 30 (1955), pp. 351–88.

2   O'Hagan, *Essays*, pp. 141–2.

3   Ellis, 'American Catholics', p. 23. The page reference is to the online version available at http://www.bc.edu/content/dam/files/offices /mission/pdf1/cu25.pdf. See also J. T. Ellis, *American Catholicism* (Chicago: University of Chicago Press, 1969; 2nd ed.), pp. 149–50; B. Conniff, 'John Tracy Ellis and the Figure of the Catholic Intellectual' in *Journal of Catholic Education* vol. 10/1 (2013), pp. 76–88.

4   *The Tablet*, 17, 24 November, 1 December 1956.

5   S. Hazareesingh, *How the French Think. An Affectionate Portrait of an Intellectual People* (New York: Basic Books, 2015), p. 4.

6   Thomas Sowell has argued that a common response of 'intellectuals' is to ignore the 'angry outcries from the masses' when these occur, taking comfort in a 'superior insight' shared by other 'thinking people'. See T. Sowell, *Intellectuals and Society* (New York; Basic Books, 2009), p. 292.

7   S. Fuller, *The Sociology of Intellectual life. The Career of the Mind in and around the Academy* (London: Sage Publications, 2010); J. T. Fisher, 'Alternative Sources of Catholic Intellectual Vitality' in *U.S. Catholic Historian* vol. 13/1 (1995), pp. 81–94.

8   C. Kurzman and L. Owens, 'The Sociology of Intellectuals' in *Annual Review of Sociology* vol. 28 (2002), pp. 63–90, especially p. 63.

9   M. L. Colish, 'Catholic and Intellectual: Conjunction or Disjunction',

in J. L. Heft (ed.), *Believing Scholars: Ten Catholic Intellectuals* (New York: Fordham University Press, 2005), p. 69.

[10] See D. C. Schindler, *The Catholicity of Reason* (Grand Rapids: William B. Eerdmans, 2013), pp. 3–32.

[11] Psalms 110: 10; 118: 99.

[12] G. Schufreider, *Confessions of a Rational Mystic: Anselm's Early Writings* (West Lafayette, Purdue University Press, 1994). See also St Augustine of Hippo, *Tract on the Gospel of John* 29:6 and St Anselm, *Proslogion*, 1. 'I believe in order to understand; I understand in order to believe.'

[13] L. Perry, *Intellectual Life in America: A History* (Chicago: University of Chicago Press, 1989), p. xv.

[14] U. L. Lehner, *The Catholic Enlightenment: the Forgotten History of a Global Movement* (New York: Oxford University Press, 2016).

[15] R. S. Appleby, P. Byrne, and W. L. Portier (eds), *Creative Fidelity: American Catholic Intellectual Traditions* (Maryknoll, NY: Orbis, 2004), p. 3; J. Hitchcock, 'Postmortem on a Rebirth: the Catholic Intellectual Renaissance' in *The American Scholar* vol. 49/2 (1980), pp. 211–225; J. R. Lothian, *The Making and Unmaking of the English Catholic Intellectual Community, 1910–1950* (Notre Dame: University of Notre Dame Press, 2009); R. Royal, *A Deeper Vision: The Catholic Intellectual Tradition in the Twentieth Century* (San Francisco: Ignatius Press, 2015), p. 450.

[16] S. Kusche, 'New Media and the Novel: A Survey of Generic Trends in Contemporary Literature', in Ansgar Nunning and Kai Marcel Sicks (eds), *Turning Points: Concepts and Narratives of Change in Literature and Other Media* (Berlin: Walter de Gruyter, 2012), p. 397.

[17] See, for example, M. L. Colish, *Medieval Foundations of the Western Intellectual Tradition* (New Haven: Yale University Press, 1999).

[18] Thomas F. O'Dea, 'The Role of the Intellectual in the Catholic Tradition' in *Daedalus* vol. 101/2 (1972), pp. 151–89.

[19] *Ibid.*, p. 179.

[20] *Ibid.*, p. 181.

[21] B. Moore, *Catholics* (London: Cape, 1972). Perhaps the classic text from the contemporary period on the broader theme is P. Hebblethwaite, *The Runaway Church: Post-Conciliar Growth or Decline* (London: Collins, 1975).

[22] C. Williamson, *The History of Catholic Intellectual Life in Scotland, 1918–1965* (London: Palgrave Macmillan, 2016), pp. 145–70.

[23] D. Rigney and T. J. Hoffman, 'Is American Catholicism Anti-Intellectual?' in *Journal for the Scientific Study of Religion* vol. 32/3 (1993), pp. 211–22.

[24] *Ibid.*, p. 216.

[25] *Ibid.*, p. 220.

26 *Ibid.*, p. 221.

27 See, in particular, A. Greeley, *The Catholic Myth* (New York: Scribners, 1990), p. 155.

28 J. S. Coleman, 'Social Capital in the Creation of Human Capital' in *American Journal of Sociology* vol. 94 Supplement (1988), pp. 95–120, especially pp. 100–101 and p. 118.

29 For an interesting antipodean viewpoint on social capital, see J. D. Gowdie, 'An Australian perspective on Vatican II and Catholic education' in Sean Whittle (ed.), *Vatican II and New Thinking about Catholic Education: The Impact and Legacy of Gravissimum Educationis* (London: Routledge, 2017), pp. 44–45.

30 A. B. Morris, 'Some social benefits of English Catholic schools' in *International Studies in Catholic Education* vol. 6/1 (2014), pp. 75–90, especially 85–86.

31 Mark Massa SJ's challenging and thought-provoking keynote address to the third Catholic Higher Education Collaborative Conference, co-sponsored by Boston College and Fordham University, makes significant related points: M. Massa, 'Keynote Address' in *Journal of Catholic Education* vol. 15/1 (2011), pp. 95–102, especially pp. 96 and 100.

32 A. S. Sassoon, 'The People, Intellectuals and Specialised Knowledge', in J. Martin (ed.), *Antonio Gramsci: Critical Assessment of Leading Political Philosophers. Volume 3: Intellectuals, Culture and the Party* (London: Routledge, 2002), pp. 94–123.

33 H. A. Giroux, *Teachers as Intellectuals: Toward a Critical Pedagogy of Learning* (Westport: Bergin and Garvey, 1988), especially p. 110. The specific trio of words quoted here is taken from the original dust-jacket.

34 Congregation for Catholic Education, *Educating Today and Tomorrow: A Renewing Passion* (2014). It needs to be stressed that, as an *instrumentum laboris*, this is a working document intended for discussion and does not represent a final authoritative promulgation on its themes.

35 *Ibid.*

36 L. E. Lynch, 'Intellectual Curiosity in Catholic Schools', in J. Stanley Murphy (ed.), *Christianity and Culture* (Baltimore: Helicon Press, 1960), pp. 62–76.

37 M. Kirwan, 'Theology and Education', in Whittle (ed.), *Vatican II*, pp. 159–70, especially 159–60.

38 See R. Topping, *Happiness and Wisdom: Augustine's Early Theology of Education* (Washington DC: Catholic University of America Press, 2012), p. 17.

39 B. P. McGuire, *Friendship and Community. The Monastic Experience 350–1250* (Ithaca: Cornell University Press, 2010), p. 295; J. Leclercq, *The Love of Learning and the Desire for God: A Study of Monastic Culture* (New York: Fordham University Press, 1974, 2nd ed.).

40 M. Higton, *A Theology of Higher Education* (New York: Oxford University Press, 2012), pp. 13–41.

41 See A. J. Cernera and O. J. Morgan, 'Learning in the Catholic Intellectual Tradition', in A. J. Cernera and O. J. Morgan (eds.), *Examining the Catholic Intellectual Tradition. Volume 2: Issues and Perspectives* (Fairfield: Sacred Heart University Press, 2002), pp. 207–224.

42 J.-P. Jossua, *Pour une histoire religieuse de l'expérience littéraire*, tome 3 (Paris: Beauchesne, 1994), pp. 289–290.

43 J. V. Schall, *The Mind that is Catholic* (Washington, DC: Catholic University of America Press, 2008), p. 5.

44 S. D. Seay, 'For the Defense and Beauty of the Catholic Faith: The Rise of Neo-Scholasticism among European Catholic Intellectuals, 1824–1879' in *Logos* vol. 5/3 (2002), pp. 131–146.

45 Pope Francis, *Evangelii Gaudium*, (2013), III:39.

46 See the related comments in M. M. Morey and J. J. Piderit, *Catholic Higher Education: A Culture in Crisis* (New York: Oxford University Press, 2006), pp. 309–310.

47 See J. Jensen, 'Questioning the social powers of art: toward a pragmatic aesthetics' in *Critical Studies in Mass Communication* vol. 12/4 (1995), pp. 365–379.

48 R. Wuthnow, *All In Sync: How Music and Art are revitalizing American Religion* (Berkeley: University of California Press, 2003); M. J. Bauer, *Arts Ministry: Nurturing the Creative Life of God's People* (Grand Rapids: William B Eerdmans, 2013); S. Flynn, 'The transformative power of art: grace outpoured', in G. Kelly and K. Saunders, *Dominican Approaches in Education* (Adelaide: ATF Press, 2014), pp. 353–63.

49 J. MacMillan, 'God, Theology and Music' in *New Blackfriars* vol. 81/947 (2000), pp. 16–26, especially p. 25. See also S. Kingsbury, 'Aesthetic Meaning in the Congregational Masses of James MacMillan' in *Yale Journal of Music and Religion* vol. 2/1 (2016), pp. 79–100.

50 U. M. Cadegan, 'The Cliff and the Tower: Reflections on the Past Half-Century in Light of the Past Half-Millennium (or so)', in J. L. Heft and U. M. Cadegan (eds), *In the Lógos of Love: Promise and Predicament in Catholic Intellectual Life* (New York: Oxford University Press, 2016), pp. 11–31. See also A. Helpi, 'The Catholic Presence in American Culture' in *American Literary History* vol. 11/1 (1999), pp. 196–212.

51 J. T. Fisher and M. M. McGuinness, 'The Catholic Intellectual Tradition: A Classification and a Calling', in J. T. Fisher and M. M..McGuinness (eds), *The Catholic Studies Reader* (New York: Fordham University Press, 2011), p. 59.

52 A. Jacobs, 'What became of the Christian intellectuals?' in *Harper's Magazine*, September 2016, pp. 54–60.

53   A. G. Sertillanges, *The Intellectual Life: Its Spirit, Conditions, Methods* (Washington: Catholic University of America Press, 1987).

54   J. Turner, 'Catholic Intellectual Traditions and Contemporary Scholarship' in *Journal of Catholic Education* vol. 2/1 (1998), pp. 35–45; J. J. Piderit and M. M. Morey (eds), *Teaching the Tradition: Catholic Themes in Academic Disciplines* (New York: Oxford University Press, 2012).

55   R. Convery, L. Franchi, and R. McCluskey, *Reclaiming the Piazza: Catholic Education as a Cultural Project* (Leominster: Gracewing, 2014), pp. 40–41.

CATHOLIC SCHOOLS AND THE NEW EVANGELISATION

Leonardo Franchi

A STRIKING FEATURE OF the contemporary Catholic cultural landscape in the West is the low level of actual religious practice. This sociological phenomenon has important repercussions for the theme of the present book. In England and Wales, for example, recently published research shows that 48.5% of the population has 'no religion'. More strikingly, the same report shows that 59.6% of cradle Catholics 'never, or practically never' attend Church.[1] If we assume that 'cradle Catholics' have attended a Catholic school, we must face up to the uncomfortable truth that attendance at a Catholic school does not seem to have had much of an influence on future religious practice. Such data is especially poignant given that we are living in the era of the New Evangelisation. We might be tempted to ask how Catholic schools can play a fruitful part in the New Evangelisation when it appears that they have not been too successful in preparing pupils for an active life of faith at the heart of the world.

In sketching out a response to this issue, we must focus first on the 'double identity' of the Catholic school as ecclesial body and civic institution. Indeed, the Catholic school as the site of meaningful intercultural dialogue is an emerging theme in Catholic education.[2] This leads to some crucial questions which require addressing:

- how can the Catholic school be a place of evangelisation when it is also a public space for dialogue?

- to what extent can the Catholic school be a site of the New Evangelisation when the pupil population is not uniformly Catholic?

- is an explicit focus on evangelisation appropriate for a civic space populated by such a diverse range of people?

Such challenging questions cannot be readily accommodated in simplistic visions of Catholic education which are tied to a 'Catholic schools for Catholic children' model. More seriously, it is all too easy to talk of the 'Catholic ethos' and 'Gospel values' in broad terms while lacking the will to address the real cultural challenges which Catholic education faces in the low levels of religious practice and lack of a shared understanding of the aims and purpose of the Catholic school in a pluralist society. There is a need, therefore, to examine what the public face of the Catholic school looks like, energised as it should be by adherence to an established set of inherited educational traditions.[3]

In the present chapter I propose that the relationship between Catholic schools and the New Evangelisation is a case-study of how an evangelising and confident Church relates positively to the complexities of belief and culture found in a plural society. The Catholic school's principal contribution to the New Evangelisation lies hence in the distinctive educational experience it offers and its mode of operation as a 'centre' of Catholic social teaching. As such, it is important to make a virtue of those elements which support and give expression to such distinctiveness while avoiding any sense that our schools' commitment to the New Evangelisation suggests a retreat behind the walls of theological and cultural defensiveness.

Catholic Schools: a Distinctive Educational Experience

For Richard Rymarz, there are five foundational principles of the New Evangelisation in Catholic schools:

1. Human witness and the need for critical mass;

2. A need to revitalise and reconceptualise religious education;

3. Celebrate the distinctiveness of Catholicism;

4. Segmented ministry and creating community and spaces for the New Evangelisation;

5. Reach out to parents and be prepared to try new strategies.[4]

Rymarz's propositions offer a fine entry-point into debates on the nature of Catholic schools. At the risk of fracturing the integrity of this 'charter', I will focus here on the 'distinctiveness of Catholicism' (no. 3) and ask what this means in a pluralist social, cultural and educational environment.[5]

A key mark of the New Evangelisation in the life of the Catholic school is that it must be both explicitly and implicitly distinctive. Explicit distinctiveness will be articulated in the first place by a cherishing of the more obvious signs of Catholic vitality: a clear and unambiguous mission statement; staff personally supportive of the mission of the school (Ryamarz's 'critical mass'); an institutional commitment to serve the poor and disadvantaged; the visibility of tasteful religious symbolism; the presence of a committed Chaplain; a well-appointed oratory (with the Blessed Sacrament reserved); regular opportunities for Mass and confession and, not least, excellent resources for the Religious Education curriculum. Arguments in support of such necessary practices are well served in the teaching of the Holy See and in the wider literature on Catholic education. They need no further comment here.[6]

Implicit distinctiveness, on the other hand, suggests neither a watering down of authentic Catholic identity nor a lessening of the pastoral energy which marks the life of the good Catholic school community. On the contrary, it is a necessary complement to the array of measures outlined above and is marked by the potential to attract those attached to other ways of understanding education. To use the language of educational 'outcomes', Catholic schools aim to shape young people who are virtuous, religiously literate, knowledgeable, formed in integrity and ready for service to the common good. For those pupils who are Catholic, we add an awareness of the intrinsic value of the lay apostolate, the need for ongoing spiritual formation and a love of authentic Catholic culture.[7]

Alongside such pupil-focussed ambitions, the Catholic school expresses its unique identity by showing how Catholic social teaching underpins its corporate life. As an 'employer' inhabiting a civic space, the Catholic school should be a first-class example of ethical and socially just practices in how staff are managed.

The key to successful integration of the explicit and implicit distinctiveness of the Catholic school is the quality of its leadership. If the Catholic school is to serve as a resource for the New Evangelisation, school leaders must recognise that their mission cannot be restricted to putting into practice an educational agenda shaped by the currently fashionable ideologies favoured by the nation state. In 2001, for example, Gerald Grace referred to the 'mission integrity' of Catholic schools threatened, as they were and are, by the rapid advance of market forces. Such a pursuit of materialist interests, he argued, could not sit easily beside a Catholic school's commitment to pursuing spiritual and moral interests.[8] Leadership in the Catholic school hence assumes a commitment to the New Evangelisation by showing how a Catholic vision of the human person and society underpins the life of the school community.

Distinctive Leadership in Catholic Education

The early years of the twenty-first century have seen 'educational leadership' emerge at the forefront of the policy agenda.[9] As Catholic schools operate in civic society, there should be no opt-out from this direction of travel. Few people would argue with the proposition that effective leadership is essential for the development of successful schools.[10] We now need a renewed commitment to ascertaining what effective leadership in Catholic schools entails.[11]

Leadership in Catholic education should not be restricted to discussion on the role of the named school leader (Principal) and the duties of those in some way responsible for the day-to-day management of the school. The Catholic school leader, rather, models a professional identity which is rooted in an authentically Catholic understanding of education and not in secularist ideologies. Given the Church's long history as provider of education, there is a considerable 'back catalogue' of philosophical and theological material on which to draw for inspiration.[12]

In his influential theological volume, *Models of the Church*, Avery Cardinal Dulles explored in considerable detail what he had identified as the strengths and limitations of various 'models' of the Church. These models, he argued, influence how the Church is perceived by both the baptised and wider society.[13] The book repays a careful reading and Catholic educationalists can come to their own conclusions re the transferability of the ecclesiological models to Catholic school governance. The chapter on the 'Church as Institution', for example, brings into sharp relief a tension between authority as power and authority as service, with the latter deemed more in keeping with a Christian spirit. This approach can serve as a baseline to inform thinking about leadership in Catholic schools.

In developing this line of thinking, Dulles suggested that an overly sharp focus on 'Church as institution' could easily promote torpor and passivity in those not at the top, so to speak: this is not, and cannot be, a satisfactory articulation of the dynamism which should underpin the life of the Church. In other words, the concentration of 'power' in the hands of a small number of people whose decisions affect much larger numbers is, in general terms, an unhealthy model of leading any organisation, far less a Church founded on a Gospel of love.

It is worth reflecting further on what Dulles' approach means for models of leadership in Catholic schools. Given the civic nature of the Catholic school, the established social doctrine of the Church has something important to say on the question of public profile. The principle of subsidiarity, central to the established corpus of Catholic social teaching, shines a clear light on how we 'see' authority, where it is located, by whom it should be exercised, and how. Subsidiarity, properly understood and exercised, should ensure that 'higher-level social authority' (the state) does not damage the rights of individuals to fulfil their civic duties.[14] This offers a suitable frame for the discussion of models of leadership which are, in keeping with the analysis of Dulles (above), open to dialogue and suspicious of a rigid over-centralisation of authority.

To counter any shift towards a heavily centralised management structure, and in recognition of the vital principle of subsidiarity, we need a renewed focus on the Catholic school as a community of educators where leadership and responsibility are truly shared, as appropriate, among the staff. While we should be wary of importing pre-packaged models of leadership into the life of the Catholic school, it is possible to assess what can be learned from ideas already in circulation.

The emergence of so-called Distributed Leadership appears to offer us some way ahead. Distributed Leadership refers to ways of managing which, unsurprisingly, lessen the organisational focus on a single leader, or sets of leaders.[15] It is, by definition, collegial. The popular use of the term 'collegial' in everyday discourse reflects a desire for some form of shared ownership of decisions: we do like to feel that we have had some say in the formulation of decisions which affect our working life and professional identity. Accusations of non-collegial ways of working are hence very serious! At its best, Distributed Leadership is neither an unwillingness to make decisions nor an expression of a tiredness manifested in getting others to do what the leader should ordinarily be doing. On the contrary, a confident leader recognises the gifts and talents of all colleagues and wishes to harness these abilities for the common good. To give a very brief example, a Head Teacher should not normally make decisions about content of individual courses but, at the same time, needs to oversee mechanisms for wider quality control. The relationship between the Head Teacher and the teacher in charge of a curriculum and/or a particular department is, hence, flexible and based on mutual respect.

Of course, caution is needed. If, for example, Distributed Leadership were intended as a corrective to the perceived predominance of autocratic management styles, there is no reason to suppose that those to whom leadership is distributed will automatically adopt a more collegial style. This could lead to a position in which a team of 'autocrats' fight for supremacy. This is a recipe for systemic chaos.

The notion of Servant Leadership would seem to offer a practical and personalised avenue for the operation of Distributed Leadership.[16] Servant Leadership seems to turn on its head the notion of the leader as a form of chief executive of an educational community. A Servant Leader, ideally, should not wish to centralise decision-making or form management teams which resemble an echo chamber. Leadership, rather, is shared and demonstrated in service to others. The Servant Leader is the one who leads by example, eschews the privileges traditionally associated with management and works within the four leadership frames viz.: 'vision, credibility, trust and service'.[17]

The understanding of leadership as a professional disposition of the Catholic teacher does not mean that any practising teacher, no matter how proficient in classroom teaching duties, would make a competent school leader. The link between Distributed Leadership and Servant Leadership is located in the intersection of vision and management: all Catholic teachers should share in the vision of Catholic education and are called to be visionary in how they lead pupils, colleagues and parents towards the ambitious goals of the school. In this respect, all teachers lead through their various ways of articulating the concepts of 'vision, credibility, trust and service' (see above) in the particular role assigned to them in the life of the school.

As servant, the Catholic leader is both manager and visionary. If we see management as the maintenance and promotion of order, the visionary aspect has an eye on development and reform, as necessary.[18] This is a high tariff for leaders in any organisation and demands a substantial degree of energy, resilience and courage in the face of challenges from other educational currents.

But, we might ask, are these (and other) leadership theories no more than fads which in due course will be more fuel to the already blazing bonfire of failed educational projects? While there is little to be gained in looking too far ahead given the pace of change in education today, a form of Distributed Leadership, allied to Servant Leadership, offers the seeds of a fresh framework for supporting and developing leaders in Catholic schools.[19] In this light, the distribution of leadership in Catholic schools should not be framed primarily as response to a particular leadership theory or as an example of an individual's preferred management style. It is, in fact, an expression of the apostolate of the lay people who are called to find holiness in their particular vocation.[20] Catholic teachers, occupying a privileged position at the heart of the Church and in the middle of the world, have a unique opportunity to live the lay vocation in a truly prophetic manner. They are called, no less, to make the New Evangelisation a reality in the midst of the ecclesial and civic space known as the Catholic school. In so doing, the wider Church has an opportunity to observe and learn from the corps of Catholic teachers just what it means to transform the world through professional work done in the proper spirit.

For this to happen, however, what is needed is not a rush towards MBA style leadership courses. We must, rather, find the resources to support the theological and pastoral formation of teachers.

Theological Formation and the Vocation to Holiness

A feature of the New Evangelisation is the indispensable focus on reinvigoration of the missionary impulses of the Church. The lay Catholic is called to holiness and a life of virtue. There is a pressing need to refresh our understanding of how to make the lay apostolate something attractive in itself and not just a way of assisting the clergy in parish duties. To be clear, the lay apostolate aims to transform the world through a commitment to living our familial, social and professional obligations in a truly Christian spirit.[21]

The scope of the lay apostolate is immense. It is much more than the assumption of liturgical functions viz. Reader/Extraordinary Minister of Holy Communion. While such roles are important to the life of the Church, they by no means exhaust the scope of lay apostolate. Indeed too strong a focus on parish involvement could, potentially, limit our apostolic endeavours if it reduced the time available for family duties and keeping up with friends.[22]

The Catholic teacher, as one of the baptised, is called to sanctity in the fulfilment of professional duties. Of course, discussion on the role and mission of the lay person in education cannot ignore the decline of religious orders and congregations with a special charism for education.[23] This is not the place to explore the 'hows' and 'whys' of this phenomenon.[24] Suffice it to say that few Catholic schools today have other than a lay teaching profile. It would be wrong to hark back to a mythical golden age when Catholic schools were staffed primarily by members of such orders/congregations. What matters now is avoiding any sense that the lay Catholic teacher is no more than a replacement for the supposed ideal of a teacher from a religious order or congregation.

We must also ask how the Catholic teacher, not just the school leader, integrates the universal call to holiness with the need for professional excellence. An important feature of policy discussions around school effectiveness is the question of teacher expertise. To what extent, if at all, are the knowledge levels, attitudinal dispositions and personality quirks of teachers related to student achievement?[25] Indeed, can the wider question of pupils' future religious practice be classed under the aims of the school?

It goes without saying that Catholic educators must engage positively with research and scholarly discussions on all aspects of what is often called 'school improvement'. A Catholic school must be striving for excellence in all it does: that is part and parcel of the processes of dialogue and encounter mentioned above. The teacher in the Catholic school, however, must bring to the table the need for ongoing, systematic and meaningful theological formation of staff. This is one area where the distinctiveness of the Catholic school should be evident.

Why is this the case? To return to first principles, Catholic theology supports an understanding of 'Catholic anthropology' which, in turn, is the base for an authentic philosophy of Catholic education. Therefore, the Catholic educator, and not just the specialist teacher of Religious Education, must grow ever more aware of how Catholic theological principles underpin and give life to his/her ongoing professional formation.

A classic definition of theology is 'faith seeking understanding'. To have the gift of faith is not to act with absolute certainty but always to seek advice, illumination and enlightenment. Prayer is at the heart of the process. 'Faith seeking understanding' also merits revisiting from an educational angle. The tense of the verb 'seeking' is the present continuous, thus showing that the study of theology, like the development of so-called professional knowledge, is ongoing. To be clear, 'seeking understanding' is the leitmotif of the Catholic educational project.

The need for professional and religious formation of teachers was recognised by the Congregation for Catholic Education in *Lay Catholics in Schools: Witnesses to Faith*, published in 1982.[26] The importance given in the document to 'permanent formation' reflects a general uneasiness in Church circles about the demographic change in the nature of the Catholic teaching force in the years following the Second Vatican Council. As noted above, the salient feature was the gradual replacement of teachers from Religious Orders and Congregations with lay staff. There was concern that the new corps of lay teachers might not have as sufficiently strong a grasp of the Church's theological and educational traditions as did teachers from dedicated Orders/Congregations.

The importance of formation was central to another document of the Congregation for Catholic Education, *The Religious Dimension of Education in a Catholic School*, published in 1988. This important contribution explored the necessity of solid teacher formation in both human and religious qualities.[27] The desired unity of vision lends credibility to the mission of the school as a place of human and religious formation. Regarding 'preparation', the document had some strong words to say about the 'Religion teacher' but the concern expressed over the effects caused by the 'unprepared teacher' could be equally applied to any teacher in the Catholic school: 'to do a great deal of harm', as noted in paragraph 97 is indeed a strong accusation.

The importance of rigorous theological formation for teachers was again emphasised by the Congregation for Catholic Education in 1992.[28] *Educating Together in Catholic Schools: A Shared Mission between Consecrated Persons and the Lay Faithful* dealt expressly with the need for wider professional formation for all educators and called specifically for 'an opportune formational theological itinerary'. Reflection on this advice reminds us of the specific vocation to teach. To be a Christian is to accept the call to evangelise and teach others but to do so as a lay person immersed in worldly affairs. Theological knowledge needs the complement of suitable spiritual formation if it is to avoid an overly cognitive approach to formation.

These paragraphs are prophetic. Indeed they are as relevant today as when they were first written. The emphasis on 'permanent formation' is very much part of the wider educational establishment's vocabulary. What is now to be decided is how best to support and find resources for this ongoing process of formation.

In the Apostolic Exhortation *Evangelii Gaudium* (The Joy of the Gospel), Pope Francis offers advice on how to be an effective evangelising community. He recognises the role of the Catholic school as a 'valuable resource' for the New Evangelisation but stops short of giving specific recommendations on how the relationship could be developed.[29] Given the multiplicity of socio-political contexts in which Catholic schools operate, this seems a sensible position to adopt.

In this light, teacher formation processes, both pre-service and in professional contexts, necessarily vary across the universal Church. Nonetheless, it is time to take seriously the need for some form of universal 'action plan' which sketches out broad lines of engagement but leaves sufficient space for local initiatives. This is a question for particular churches to address but which could lead to new forms of national and international collaboration in both online and traditional forms of education.

Concluding Remarks

The emphasis on ongoing theological formation, while central to the life of the Catholic school, is also a marker of a wider aim: the need to develop the expertise of lay people in theology. The Church of the New Evangelisation can only move forward with a shared commitment to the formation of all the baptised.

The chapter has explored aspects of how the Catholic school can contribute towards the New Evangelisation. It has argued that the distinctiveness of Catholic schools must be evident in both its preferred models of leadership and in commitment to the theological formation of teachers. Implicit in these arguments is the hope that the energy and vision underpinning these initiatives will spill over into the life of the wider Church. If we make our schools such centres of excellence in governance, we invite people to 'come and see' why we do what we do.

To conclude, I offer below four areas which show how the arguments presented in the present chapter could have wider positive outcomes for the Church and society.

1. In dealing with issues of leadership in Catholic schools, there emerge opportunities for reflection on how lay people can make a positive contribution to contemporary society and to the life of the Church. The lay person is called to lead society in charity and hope. To see such charity and hope in action in normal life is to work for the New Evangelisation.

2. Servant Leadership is an acting out of Catholic social teaching. To serve, therefore, is to act as the foundation, or pillar of a good society. The foundation might be unseen but without it no structure would exist. Its expression in the Catholic school should be recognised across wider educational systems as something intrinsic to the operation of any good school.

3. The leader of a Catholic school must see beyond simply 'looking after the interests of the Church' if that is understood solely in a narrow institutionalised manner. Similarly, the lay person is not called to be a representative of the Bishops in civil society. The call to holiness is a call to act freely as leaven in secular society.

4. All lay people should have opportunities for systematic theological development. While this should be a professional requirement for the teacher in a Catholic school, the wider Church has a responsibility to ensure that ongoing formation

is adequately provided at a local level. It is fair to say that we have not yet managed to find ways in which this could be made attractive to those who attend Church regularly but do not avail themselves of any means of formation.

These are exciting times for the Church. As the New Evangelisation is an open project (without fixed time limits) we can find inspiration in the possibilities offered by the worldwide network of Catholic schools. While the family is necessarily at the centre of the New Evangelisation, the Catholic school is a sufficiently robust complement operating at the frontier between Church and wider society. As such, the time and energy given to improving the life of the Catholic school is indeed time very well spent.

Notes

1   Benedict XVI Centre for Religion and Society, *Contemporary Catholicism in England and Wales*, 2016.

2   Congregation for Catholic Education, *Educating for Intercultural Dialogue in Catholic Schools: Living in Harmony for a Civilization of Love*, 2013.

3   L. Franchi, 'The Catholic School as a Courtyard of the Gentiles' in *Journal of Catholic Education* vol. 17/2 (2014), online.

4   R. Rymarz, *The New Evangelization: Issues and Challenges for Catholic Schools* (Queensland: Connor Court Publishing, 2013).

5   Although I will refer to 'Catholic schools' throughout the chapter, the issues raised can be equally applied to Catholic colleges and universities.

6   Congregation for Catholic Education, *The Religious Dimension of Education in a Catholic School*, 1988. See also J. Piderit, and M. Morey, M. (Eds.), *Teaching the Tradition: Academic Themes in Academic Disciplines* (Oxford: Oxford University Press, 2012).

7   R. Convery, L. Franchi, and R. McCluskey, *Reclaiming the Piazza: Catholic Education as a Cultural Project*. (Leominster: Gracewing, 2013).

8   G. Grace, 'The State and Catholic Schooling in England and Wales: Politics, Ideology and Mission Integrity' in *Oxford Review of Education* vol. 27/4 (2001), pp. 489–500.

9   There is a plethora of material available on what constitutes good educational leadership. An introduction to the field is found in J. O'Brien, D. Murphy, J. Draper, C. Forde & M. McMahon, *School Leadership*. (Edinburgh: Dunedin Academic Press, 2016).

[10] J. O'Brien and D. Murphy, 'Leadership, School Leadership and Headship' in J. O'Brien, et al. (Ed.) *School Leadership*, pp. 1–29.

[11] Cf. A. Havard, *Virtuous Leadership* (New York: Scepter, 2007) and G. Grace, 'Faith School Leadership: A Neglected Sector of In-Service Education in the United Kingdom' in *Professional Development in Education* vol. 35/3 (2009), pp. 485–494.

[12] See for example St Benedict of Nursia (480 AD to 547 AD), the founder of the Benedictines, who gave a list of recommendations for the abbots of monasteries. His advice for leaders to be both flexible and firm remains valid today: http://www.documentacatholicaomnia.eu/03d/0480–0547,_Benedictus_Nursinus,_Regola,_EN.pdf.

[13] A. Dulles, *Models of the Church* (New York: Doubleday, 2002.)

[14] Pontifical Council for Justice and Peace, *Compendium of the Social Doctrine of the Church*. 2005, 187.

[15] For a review of the current literature on Distributed Leadership, see A. Harris, 'Introduction'. In A. Harris (Ed.), *Distributed Leadership: Different Perspectives* (London: Springer, 2009.)

[16] For a brief survey of the history of Servant-Leadership, see T. Kaetkaew Punnachet, 'Catholic Servant-Leadership in Education: Going Beyond the Secular Paradigm' in *International Studies in Catholic Education* volume 1/2 (2009), pp. 117–134.

[17] J. Nsiah and K. Walker, *The Servant: Leadership Roles of Catholic High School Principals* (Rotterdam: Sense Publishers, 2016) pp. 133.

[18] A. Dosen, 'Leadership in a Catholic Key' in A. Dosen, and B. Rieckhoff, (eds.), *Catholic School Leadership* (Charlotte NC: Information Age Publishing, 2016), pp. 1–18.

[19] R. Coll, 'Catholic School Leadership: Exploring Its Impact on the Faith Development of Probationer Teachers in Scotland' in *International Studies in Catholic Education* vol. 1/2 (2009), pp. 200–213.

[20] Pope John Paul II, *Christifidelis Laici* (1988).

[21] *Ibid.*

[22] 'He waits for us every day, in the laboratory, in the operating theatre, in the army barracks, in the university chair, in the factory, in the workshop, in the fields, in the home and in all the immense panorama of work. Understand this well: there is something holy, something divine, hidden in the most ordinary situations, and it is up to each one of you to discover it.' J. Escriva, *Conversations with Mgr Escriva*. (London: Scepter, 1980), p. 114.

[23] Cf. Congregation for Catholic Education, *Lay Catholics in Schools: Witnesses to Faith*, 1982 and *Educating Together in Catholic Schools: A Shared Mission between Consecrated Persons and the Lay Faithful*, 2007.

[24] Cf. T. O'Donoghue, *Come Follow Me and Forsake Temptation-Catholic Schooling and the Retention of Teachers for Religious Teaching Orders, 1922–1965* (Berne: Peter Lang, 2004) and *Catholic Teaching Brothers: Their Life in the English-Speaking World 1891–1965* (New York: Palgrave Macmillan, 2013).

25   One wonders what contemporary educational policy makers would
      make of the 'quirkiness' of the fictional Miss Jean Brodie: 'Art and
      religion first; then philosophy; lastly science. That is the order of the
      great subjects of life, that's their order of importance'. M. Spark, *The
      Prime of Miss Jean Brodie* (London: Penguin Books, 1965), p. 25.

26   'Permanent formation involves a wide variety of different elements;
      a constant search for ways to bring it about is therefore required of
      both individuals and the community. Among the variety of means
      for permanent formation, some have become ordinary and virtually
      indispensable instruments: reading periodicals and pertinent books,
      attending conferences and seminars, participating in workshops,
      assemblies and congresses, making appropriate use of periods of
      free time for formation. All lay Catholics who work in schools should
      make these a habitual part of their own human, professional, and
      religious life.' Congregation for Catholic Education, *Lay Catholics in
      Schools: Witnesses to Faith*, para. 74.

27   'In this area, especially, an unprepared teacher can do a great deal of
      harm. Everything possible must be done to ensure that Catholic
      schools have adequately trained religion teachers; it is a vital necessity
      and a legitimate expectation.' Congregation for Catholic Education,
      The Religious Dimension of Education in a Catholic School, para. 97.

28   'The transmission of the Christian message through teaching implies
      a mastery of the knowledge of the truths of the faith and of the
      principles of spiritual life that require constant improvement. This
      is why both consecrated and lay educators of the Catholic school
      need to follow an opportune formational theological itinerary. Such
      an itinerary makes it easier to combine the understanding of faith
      with professional commitment and Christian action. Apart from
      their theological formation, educators need also to cultivate their
      spiritual formation in order to develop their relationship with Jesus
      Christ and become a Master like Him. In this sense, the formational
      journey of both lay and consecrated educators must be combined
      with the moulding of the person towards greater conformity with
      Christ (cf. *Rm* 8:29) and of the educational community around Christ
      the Master. Moreover, the Catholic school is well aware that the
      community that it forms must be constantly nourished and com-
      pared with the sources from which the reason for its existence
      derives: the saving word of God in Sacred Scripture, in Tradition,
      above all liturgical and sacramental Tradition, enlightened by the
      Magisterium of the Church.' Congregation for Catholic Education,
      *Educating Together in Catholic Schools: A Shared Mission between
      Consecrated Persons and the Lay Faithful*. 2002, para. 26.

29   Pope Francis, Apostolic Exhortation *Evangelii Gaudium*, para. 134.

PART 2

CATHOLIC EDUCATION AND THE NEW EVANGELISATION: PRACTICAL APPLICATIONS

THE UNIVERSITY CHAPLAIN: HIGHER EDUCATION, STUDENT LIFE AND THE NEW EVANGELISATION

Bishop John Keenan

W HEN I WAS young my uncle John, a joyful, old Jesuit brother, would make his annual family visit to our home. His arrival was always greeted with joy in the family because he was able to tell us the best stories we had ever heard, tales that, no matter how often we had heard them, still drew us into the scene as though we were there. The outcome had us invariably splitting our sides with laughter. It was in his nature to be playful and to pull our legs and he never failed to catch us out. Once, when I was well ensconced in my university years, he looked sternly at me and asked, 'John, are you keeping the faith?' I replied, with the immediacy of someone caught like a rabbit in headlights, 'Oh yes, Brother John, I am', thereby falling perfectly into the trap he had so masterfully set. His face brightened cheerfully in the triumph of someone who had 'got me' and he mischievously concluded, 'Well you shouldn't be keeping it, you should be spreading it.'

The task of New Evangelisation is quite simply to proclaim the Gospel or spread the faith wherever we are. Blessed Paul VI established clearly and firmly the benchmark of all evangelisation when he laid down the maxim that 'there can be no evangelisation without the explicit proclamation of Jesus as Lord'.[1] In this way he made it clear that evangelisation cannot be confused with a vague humanitarian desire to make the world a better place or simply with working for justice and human rights, or even in getting involved in bringing aid to the poor locally or globally. If it is real evangelisation then proclaiming Jesus Christ has somehow to be its beginning and end and *raison d'être*. It means that we want to make the world a better place because we love Jesus and we know that, whatever else we do to improve our planet, it has to involve telling those we meet about Jesus so that He can take His place as Lord of Creation and History and become the Lord of their lives too. Of course it also means giving silent witness by the good example of our Christian lives of virtue but our Christian imperative to spread the Good News cannot be satisfied until the Gospel flows out of our mouths and this applies irrespective of the *milieu* in which the particular Church exists, whether it be out on a mission in the developing world or in the campuses and lecture halls of universities.

Perhaps this is as good a place as any for debunking the urban myth that seems to have sprung up everywhere. I am talking about the often quoted words of Saint Francis of Assisi that Christians should preach the Gospel every-where and, if we have to, use words. In the context of evangelisation it is perhaps Saint Francis' best known contemporary pearl of wisdom, except that he probably never said it! Instead, as the other Francis—Pope Francis—emphasised, quoting Pope St John Paul II, the absolute priority of evangelisation is the 'joyful, patient and progres-sive preaching of the saving death and resurrection of Jesus Christ' and these words hold true for all of us whoever we are and wherever we live our Christian life.[2]

Of course another less attributed but just as misleading assumption that has held sway for too many centuries to count, is that evangelisation is the task of Church profes-sionals, principally the clergy and religious and, maybe, teachers, but not the competence of your regular Joe who sits in the pews for Sunday Mass and then goes back out into the world to earn his keep and raise a family. In *Evangelii Gaudium* Pope Francis reminds us that evangelisa-tion is the task of the whole Church, by which he means all of us. In virtue of our baptism all the members of the People of God have become missionary disciples.[3] He is quite clear that Jesus' mandate excludes no-one, no matter what reason might be offered: 'All the baptised, whatever their position in the Church or their level of instruction in the faith, are agents of evangelisation'.[4] To emphasise the point he stresses how we can no longer look back fondly to the days when religious orders would come and give parish missions to refresh the rest of us or to harp back after some similar 'plan of evangelisation to be carried out by professionals while the rest of the faithful are simply passive recipients.'[5] New Evangelisation is about you and me and every one of us, each of us as a matter of habit evangelising each other and our own surroundings. The simple fact of New Evangelisation is that

> every Christian is challenged, here and now, to be actively engaged in evangelisation... Every Christian is a missionary to the extent that he or she has encountered the love of God in Christ Jesus. We no longer say that there are disciples and there are missionaries, but rather that we are always 'missionary disciples'.[6]

What qualifies us to be evangelisers is not a degree from a University or ordination by the bishop but the simple fact that we have been baptised like Jesus with a mission to bring the Good News to the poor and have 'truly experienced God's saving love'.[7] To have really met Jesus is to want to tell others about Him and, in fact 'it does not need much time or lengthy training to go out and proclaim that love'.[8]

All we have to do is to turn to the Gospels to see how those who failed to pass on the joy of their meeting with Jesus had not, for all they had been in His presence and even conversed with Him, really encountered Jesus. We can think of the rich young man who was so trapped in his wealth that he left his meeting with Jesus sad and silent and we never hear of him again. More often than not, thankfully, we read of authentic encounters with Jesus that transform those who meet Him, there and then, into missionary disciples. As Pope Francis argues, 'If we are not convinced, let us look at those first disciples, who, immediately after encountering the gaze of Jesus, went forth to proclaim joyfully: "We have found the Messiah!"'[9] And, just in case we imagined that a life of sin disqualified us from spreading the Good News, the Pope presents us with the figure of the Samaritan woman who had already got through five relationships and was presently living in an irregular union. She 'became a missionary immediately after speaking with Jesus and many Samaritans came to believe in him "because of the woman's testimony"'.[10]

Changes in Higher Education

Perhaps the most interesting development of New Evangelisation is its *finesse*. Though it never forgets the absolute priority to preach the name of Jesus, His Gospel and His offer of salvation, it is, for all that, perhaps a more thoughtful enterprise than it was in past times. The Church does not want to enter the scene with a pre-packaged, 'one size fits all', 'take it or leave it' approach to earthly realities that have not heard sufficiently of Jesus or understood the implications of salvation. New Evangelisation comes to enter into dialogue with culture as much as to proclaim the Good News. It comes as much to listen and understand as to speak and be heard. It comes as much to learn and grow as to teach and plant seeds. It comes to understand the particular life and *modus operandi* of each situation it enters with all its idiosyncrasies and nuances. It comes to live with people in their world in order to show them how their particular situation can be even richer. And so, just as much as the Church lives from the eternal, unchanging mystery rooted in the Trinity, we are more than ever aware that we also 'exist concretely in history as a pilgrim people'.[11]

So we have to be a people for everyone. New Evangelisation recognises that every person, scene and culture is unique. It is always aware of entering as a guest into a 'complex interweaving of personal relationships entailed in the life of a human community'.[12] So we do not enter into social institutions and their environments with the pretension of taking members from them to form them into some exclusive and elite group set apart but seek ourselves to enter into the midst of that community and become valued members among members, not apart from them but 'in the mix' as their salt, leaven and light. We can be a people for everyone and part of every culture if we remember Jesus' commission to 'Go and make disciples of all nations' and Saint Paul's challenge to be 'all things to all men' and his reminder that in the Church, 'there is neither Jew or Greek... for we are all one in Christ Jesus'.[13] The Church is for everyone and every community can be part of the Church or, at least, welcomed to cooperate and work with it in the building up of all that is true, noble, right and whatever is pure, lovely, admirable, excellent or praiseworthy.

To put it another way, 'the People of God is incarnate in the peoples of the earth, each of which has its own culture'.[14] The concept of culture is a great discovery to the theology of evangelisation in recent times. Culture has to do with the lifestyle of a given society, the specific way in which its members relate to one another, to other creatures and to God. Understood in this way, culture embraces the totality of a people's life.[15] The full implication of this reality is that there is really no one ready-made Gospel for all. It means we have to start not with a pre-packed message but with the human community and members in front of us and build our Gospel up anew from the encounter with them. As Pope Saint John Paul II put it:

> It is man in the full truth of his existence, of his personal being and also of his community and social being, this man who is the primary route that the Church must travel in fulfilling her mission: he is the primary and fundamental way for the Church, the way traced out by Christ himself, the way that leads invariably through the mystery of the Incarnation and the Redemption.[16]

The point is that Higher Education in the twenty-first century is just one such community that, like any other community, 'in the course of its history has developed its own culture with legitimate autonomy'.[17] So any effective evangelisation of University life has to mean the Church entering fully into academic life as an integral part of it and being recognised and accepted as a member of the community by those on campus in order to be the Academy's own Gospel and light. Just as this is true of the academic culture as such it is also true of each person the Church encounters within it, whether student, academic or employee because every person 'always exists in reference to their society and finds there a concrete way of relating to reality. The human person is always situated in a culture (such that) nature and culture are intimately linked'.[18] It follows that grace supposes culture, and God's gift becomes flesh in the culture of those who receive it.[19] So what is the culture of higher education today that we are called to evangelise?

You would think that the idea of a University would be basically timeless and precise. Certainly in former times it was 'what it said on the tin'. The medieval Latin word *universitatem* was itself a composition of the words: *unus,* or one, and *versus,* or turned. Put together it meant it was a place where everything was turned or pointed to a unified centre or whole. In terms of knowledge it implied a point of view, an act of faith, if you like, that behind the aggregate of all the facts of this world there was a point of meaning where everything made sense. Human existence was not fragmentary and absurd but was caught up into some ultimate purpose beyond itself. It was in virtue of this idea of wisdom alive in the heart of Europe that civilization succeeded in expressing itself in one of its most globally emblematic institutions, the university. Such a belief in meaning and its metaphysical unity attracted an assembly of like-minded academics who found themselves formed into a community of scholars with a common mission to gather knowledge from every field and so enrich its one, overarching significance. As the thirteenth and fourteenth centuries unfolded, professors, doctors, masters and students worked together in the service

of this ever-emerging meaning. It was the period in which
the expression of the unity of knowledge and learning was
assembling itself around the idea of Humanism, which was
taking shape as a successful synthesis between theological
and philosophical knowledge and other arts and sciences.
According to Pope Saint John Paul this synthesis would have
been unthinkable without Christianity and the age-old work
of evangelisation carried out by the Church in her encounter
with the multiple ethnic and cultural realities of the continent.[20] He went on to advise that, 'this remembrance of
history is indispensable in order to build the cultural perspective of the (world) of today and in the future, in whose
construction the university is called to play an irreplaceable
role.'[21] Wisdom was built slowly over centuries but, playing
their humble part in its emergence, each scholar hoped to
grow in virtue. The university was called *Alma Mater*, the
mother who would bring to birth in society an ever more
humane world. The Pope's argument was clear:

> Just as the (contemporary culture) cannot develop
> without drawing from its own roots, the same can
> be said of the university. Indeed, it is the place *par
> excellence* in which to seek the truth and make
> accurate analyses of phenomena, striving constantly
> to find more complete and fruitful syntheses. And
> just as (the modern world) cannot be reduced to a
> market, so the university cannot be subjected to the
> requirements of the social and economic fabric,
> although it must be an integral part of them, on pain
> of losing its own predominantly cultural profile.[22]

This background provides a good *locus* for reflection upon
the relationship between the university and the Church at
the beginning of the third millennium.

The Church looks to the university with respect and
confidence. For its part the Church wants to do its utmost
to offer its own multiform contribution to the Academy. As
Pope Francis has pointed out, 'proclaiming the Gospel
message to different cultures also involves proclaiming it

to professional, scientific and academic circles (and) this means an encounter between faith, reason and the sciences with a view to developing new approaches and arguments on the issue of credibility, (as well as a) creative apologetics which would encourage greater openness to the Gospel on the part of all.[23] He is not slow to see its connection with the wider enterprise of New Evangelisation. So 'when certain categories of reason and the sciences are taken up into the proclamation of the message these categories then become tools of evangelisation; water is changed into wine'.[24]

That is why, in his view, 'universities are outstanding environments for articulating and developing this evangelising commitment in an interdisciplinary and integrated way'.[25] They are, in this way, just like Catholic schools, which 'strive to join their work of education with the explicit proclamation of the Gospel, (and so) are a most valuable resource for the evangelisation of culture'.[26]

The Church attempts to carry out this task above all in the presence of teachers and students who know how to combine competence and scientific rigour with an intense spiritual life, so as to imbue the university environment with a Gospel spirit.[27] It also makes its own particular contribution to higher education through Catholic universities which carry on the heritage of the ancient universities born from the heart of the Church.

It has also begun to do so in our own times by an initiative of New Evangelisation uniquely developed in the context of the Academy, called 'cultural laboratories'. Through such cultural laboratories constructive dialogue is engaged between faith and culture and between science, philosophy and theology. At the same time ethics is seen as an intrinsic requirement of research for an authentic service to the human being.[28] In this way the Church hopes to build on the firm foundations laid and developed at the inception of European universities.

These foundations, however, are not as enduring or safe as they once were. The contemporary reality of the university is very different and has, from modernity onwards, been carving out a new purpose for itself. Now reigning is the effort to realise freedom understood as the person's unlimited right to self-creation. From this perspective universities cannot and should not profess any *a priori* truths that limit the horizon of individual choices. To fit in with this view there can be no truth in the classical sense of the word as something given in the natural order, universally and necessarily, and just to be accepted. No doubt that is what Pope John Paul was thinking about when, in a letter to the University of Glasgow in 2001 on the occasion of its 550th anniversary, he referred to 'unsettled times when the very existence of truth and the human being's capacity to know it are cast in doubt'. Perhaps he was thinking of the current climate where the only truth allowed is the truth we create for ourselves and the pragmatism that holds that the only kind of knowledge we need is that which allows some working assumptions to let us get on with things.

Such a perspective has only been exacerbated by the sheer explosion of knowledge and the 'googles' of data in recent times that have amassed to sweep away the few traditional faculties with a plethora of new colleges and schools in life-sciences, education, business and administration, technology, film and drama and so on. There is no hope, much less time, to attempt any overarching integration of all these units. Instead a juxtaposition of semi-independent institutions is the preferred or only feasible model. In short it makes little sense to talk of University anymore. Rather the preferred collective term of 'higher education' is really a proxy for the new diversity, not university, of educational enterprises.

In case discussion remains too philosophical, any genuine pastoral ministry in the Academy has to take into account the concrete circumstances in which university communities operate with all their internal and external pressures. Perhaps the most significant of these is the economic environment in which they exist from year to year. It would not be stretching the point to say that in the twenty-first century universities exist primarily as a function of the State's global economic plan and to increase its material wealth at least as importantly as conserving and developing its cultural patrimony. Modern economies need ever new technologies and so pressures increase on university managers to move resources towards science and technological research in labs and libraries at the expense of teaching time for students in lecture theatres. New technologies that come on stream as a result of such research need high-tech workers to operate them who do not have to be wise and virtuous so much as trained and efficient, and it needs lots of them. So where university students once made up ten percent or so of the population, or the elite whose vocation was to be formed to serve society as good and enlightened leaders, now political aspirations of student numbers are towards the forty per cent of the youth population needed to fill the high tech jobs market. By the force of statistical logic we surely now have to consider universities as places where excellence has given way to a milieu of near average intellectual ability.

The 'double-whammy', as you might call it, of less teaching time for an ever increasing student population is felt most chronically by academic staff. Writing in light of his own experiences as a university professor in 2004, Anthony King noted how the combined effect of, on the one hand, academics being drawn from teaching to research and, on the other, the far greater number of undergraduates entering campus, had resulted in a ratio of staff to students which had fallen from nine-to-one to nineteen-to-one. Staff in the past might have had no more than a dozen students whom they would know by name, taught in small groups and whose written assignments they oversaw. Now, at the time of King's writing, staff typically were assigned eighty students whose names they could not know. To add to the picture, where administration once accounted for five percent of an academic's time, it now accounted for around thirty to forty per cent.[29]

The Reality of Student Life Today

Neither is the impact on students, who are affected as if by domino effect, insignificant. There is a danger that many students may now regard their lecturers less as personal mentors and more as providers of a curriculum. Not just is the quality of their relationship with their scholars diminished but the quantity of teaching time is also not what it once was. Anthony King commented on how undergraduates used to be taught five courses a year for which they would submit, in total, twenty-five essays; in contrast, by 2004, their overstretched lecturers taught around four courses and required twelve pieces of work in a teaching year which had been reduced from twenty-five weeks to twenty.[30] So students do not need to study as they did in the past which frees up their time for more hours in part-time jobs in town that pay for what are now considered a range of expensive necessities beyond the limits of their loans and overdrafts. Students no longer really 'go up to university'. The reality is that they live with one foot on campus and the other on the High Street.

And why not? Few of their teachers know their name and others would not recognise their faces. Few have ever had the opportunity to suggest to students the higher purpose of study and so young minds are never enlightened to understand the important cultural value of universities in guarding human progress. If only the higher vocation of education were revealed to them their minds and hearts might rise to the noble summons to grow in wisdom, virtue and service of humanity. Who knows how many would be set free from the ubiquitous pressure to become rich and famous celebrities and set new sights on being self-sacrificing custodians of culture? Instead all they know is that the university is there as a function of the GDP of the State and, fingers crossed, to allow them to get rich into the bargain.

These practical considerations may seem somewhat unpalatable and perhaps will be thought out of place in a book that seeks to reflect on the effort of Catholic education to be open to new ideas and to engage in dialogue with other forms of education. Yet, as well as thinking about preserving our traditional (*ad intra*) mission to develop the theological knowledge and faith commitment of Catholic students, this book is keen to provoke some outward facing (*ad extra*) energy as its necessary complement and, in that respect, all of what has been said is relevant in identifying the spirituality of the contemporary university as a workplace. Authentic spirituality emerges only out of a precise reading of the signs of the times.

The Church's commitment to the New Evangelisation has the potential to give a new impetus to academic life provided that it can succeed not just in setting out some of the key lines of engagement between the ideals of evangelisation and academic life but also give some thought to the role of key personnel on the ground, in the thick of university pastoral ministry and the challenges that face them as they seek to take the concrete reality of current higher education culture beyond its present *impasse.*

The University Chaplain

Alongside students and academics on campus such a key personnel figure is the University chaplain. In fact in many of our universities it is the chaplaincy and chaplain who form the focal point of the Catholic presence and the hub of its engagement and life on campus. For these reasons its role is pivotal in the fruitfulness of the Church's presence and its evangelical effectiveness in higher education.

Where the chaplaincy has a building and a full time chaplain the Church truly becomes integral to the University's daily life and lived relationships and it is in this normal, everyday mingling that the Church has its deepest and most enduring impact. It is in this way that the Church is able to speak heart to heart or, person to person. As Pope

Francis says, 'It (then)… brings the Gospel to the people we meet, whether they be our neighbours or complete strangers, … the informal preaching which takes place in the middle of a conversation'.[31] He calls it the 'kind of preaching which falls to each of us as a daily responsibility' and allows the likes of a chaplain to be 'a disciple …. constantly ready to bring the love of Jesus to others, … unexpectedly and in any place: on the street, in a square, during work, on a journey.'[32] He concludes that this is the best path to follow for the Church as its 'seeks to experience a profound missionary renewal'.[33]

This was already the vision of Fr Jeremy Fairhead, chaplain to Oxford University at the turn of the new millennium, which he laid out in his paper *University Chaplaincy*.[34] He spelled out five key aims of the chaplaincy and chaplain, namely: Christ, community, catechesis, dialogue and proclamation.[35]

The first duty of a chaplaincy is to make Christ present. Ultimately Jesus is the one at work and, in the end, it is He who is the teacher and evangeliser of the University community. Chaplain and chaplaincy centre are merely his instruments.[36] Keeping this in mind allows the chaplaincy to develop an 'authentic spirituality, rooted in the great traditions of the past but looking forward.[37]

Keeping Christ at the centre allows all those who come seeking the face of Christ to find him through holiness, prayer, Eucharist, reconciliation and the Word of God, heard in fresh and new ways.[38] Chaplaincies, then, are places where Christ is met through these privileged channels of His presence.[39]

From this starting point the chaplain works outwards to ensure the chaplaincy is a place of community because the Eucharist is the Body of Christ of which we are members living together and this shared life is 'one of the greatest forms of catechesis and evangelisation' because it is in a communion that draws others into its midst that the Church best appears as a Sacramental sign and instrument of union with God and the unity of the human race.[40] From his own experience of chaplaincy community Fr Fairhead goes on to make the wise observations that such common living is essential to students in learning the proper living of the moral precepts of the Church which they cannot appreciate in an individualistic existence. For the chaplain personally such shared living is just as important to his real understanding of his vocation of priestly service.[41]

Chaplaincies should be places of catechesis in the broadest sense, founded upon dwelling on the Word of God and blossoming in mature spirituality. Fr Fairhead makes the crucial point, so often overlooked in recent times, that young people who are developing intellectually need to be challenged to grow in their understanding of the faith through familiarity with the rich traditions of Catholic literature and of art and music, as well as knowing how to approach contemporary issues of science and technology.[42]

Consequently chaplaincies should be places of multiple dialogues: respectful, academic and honest. There should be first of all a culture of ongoing conversation with the intellectual traditions at play in the university curriculum, a kind of dialogue *ab extra*, to allow the chaplaincy an opening into all the disciplines of learning.[43] As much as anything there should be space for students to reflect upon the relationship between faith and reason and to understand the longstanding Catholic tradition of harmony and complementarity between these two fields of knowledge and truth. This is one aspect of a more general requirement to understand our Western culture in its postmodern individualism, rationalism, political ideologies, ecology movements and advances in medicine and technology. Such openness to dialogue with contemporary culture works against the danger, ever present, to retreat into our own security and the culture of the ghetto'.[44]

Last, but not least, he lists the ongoing need for ecumenical dialogue, the developing field of interreligious conversation and the challenging demand for engagement with the margins.[45]

There is also the rich dialogue *ad intra* that Catholics at chaplaincy engage among themselves. As Fr Fairhead notes, 'the internationalisation of Universities has enabled a wealth of cultures and charismas that have enriched the Church to be in close contact'.[46] Shared experience on the basis of a common faith is the best antidote to ecclesial xenophobia.

Dialogue does not find its full voice unless it is free and confident to become proclamation but, with Pope Francis, Fr Fairhead advises that this should be characterised by prudence and patience and he gives examples from his own ministry. From my own past capacity as a Catholic Chaplain to a university, I can certainly attest to the many challenges which are inevitably thrown up for comment or action over the course of a busy academic year in a twenty-first century secular university. But there are also many opportunities for the sort of patient witness to one's faith which Pope Francis would have us display. Indeed, pastoral ministry takes its meaning from Christ as Shepherd caring for His sheep.[47] Jesus described the shepherd as one who lays down his life for the sheep.[48] He will not run away but will stand up to 'the wolves' and engage them.[49] The wolves are wrong ideas that often present themselves in sheep's clothing. In those moments the chaplaincy's pastoral ministry is also about recognising and correcting these wrong ideas. That is why the Holy Spirit inspired the Second Vatican Council to proclaim that the Church should not only minister to the believer but must also evangelise his culture.

Concluding Remarks

What has New Evangelisation to say to academic culture today? At its heart it is the genuinely human that is most threatened in what has been a generation of the most radical changes in the idea of a university since their inception. Significantly it was this charge—to serve and protect all that is truly human—that the Council placed on all believers.[50]

The struggle to find it underscores the joys and the hopes, the griefs and the anxieties of all peoples in this age and they remain, too, the joys, hopes, the griefs and anxieties of university academics, students and chaplains as they strive to serve their university communities.

In the letter to the University of Glasgow mentioned above, Pope John Paul proposed a pastoral ministry inspired by the Christian humanism that founded many of the medieval universities. This vision, he said, insisted on the primacy of the person over things, the priority of ethics over technology, and the superiority of spirit over matter. He concluded that, in the end 'the truth to which all learning looks is the truth of the human person created in the image of God, the fullness of which is found only in Jesus Christ, who fully reveals man to man'.

Notes

[1] Pope Paul VI, *Evangelii Nuntiandi* (1975), 22.
[2] Pope John Paul II, *Ecclesia in Asia* (1999); Pope Francis, *Evangelii Gaudium* (2013), 110.
[3] Pope Francis, *Evangelii Gaudium*, 120.
[4] *Ibid*.
[5] *Ibid*.
[6] *Ibid*.
[7] *Ibid*.
[8] *Ibid*.
[9] *Ibid*.
[10] *Ibid*.
[11] *Ibid*. 111.
[12] *Ibid*. 113.
[13] Philippians 4:8.
[14] Pope Francis, *Evangelii Gaudium*, 115.
[15] *Ibid*.
[16] Pope John Paul II, *Redemptor Hominis* (1979), 14.
[17] Pope Francis, *Evangelii Gaudium*, 115.
[18] *Ibid*.
[19] *Ibid*.
[20] Pope John Paul II, *Address at the World Meeting of University Teachers for Their Jubilee*, 9 September 2000, 5.

21   Pope John Paul II, *To those taking part in the European Symposium on the theme 'The University and the Church in Europe'* (19 July 2003).

22   *Ibid.*

23   Pope Francis, *Evangelii Gaudium*, 132.

24   *Ibid.*

25   *Ibid.*, 134.

26   *Ibid.*

27   *Ibid.*, 3.

28   Pope John Paul II, *Address at the World Meeting of University Teachers for Their Jubilee*, 9 September 2000, n. 5.

29   A. King, 'More and more undergraduates are being taught less and less' in *The Telegraph*, 13 January 2004.

30   *Ibid.*

31   Pope Francis, *Evangelii Gaudium*, 127.

32   *Ibid.*

33   *Ibid.*

34   Consiglio Conferenze Episcopali d'Europa, *Università e Chiesa in Europa* (Turin: Editrice Elledici, 2003).

35   *Ibid.*, p. 140.

36   *Ibid.*

37   *Ibid.*

38   *Ibid.*

39   *Ibid.*

40   *Ibid.*, p. 141.

41   *Ibid.*

42   *Ibid.*

43   *Ibid.*, p. 142.

44   *Ibid.*

45   *Ibid.*, p. 143.

46   *Ibid.*

47   John 10, passim.

48   John 10:11

49   John 10:13

50   Vatican II, *Gaudium et Spes* (7 December 1965), 1.

THE HEAD TEACHER: LEADING THE CATHOLIC SCHOOL FOR THE NEW EVANGELISATION

Isabelle Boyd

*Then Jesus again spoke to them, saying, 'I am the
Light of the world; he who follows Me will not walk
in the darkness, but will have the Light of life.'*

John 8:12.

I WAS THE HEAD Teacher of a Catholic secondary school
for 11 years. In many respects it was the most challenging—and most rewarding—job I have ever had. I had
two comic posters on display in my room. One read:
'Attention all teenagers. **No** is a complete sentence'. The
other was a caricature of the teacher with mortarboard and
cane asking the young people: 'What part of "no" didn't
you understand?' The purpose of the authors was to
emphasise the rebellion in young people to push at boundaries. After all this is the role of the young. The posters also
serve as a useful starting point for my thoughts.

These may seem harsh for one working in a caring,
nurturing Catholic community but in many ways, they
capture the key role for many of our colleagues working in
Catholic education today, and in responding to the New
Evangelisation.

Catholic schools can be at the heart of the New Evangelisation. They are certainly at the heart of community,
constancy and Church. Our children and young people live
in a throwaway society. Everything is instant, urgent and
transient. This is so often the antithesis of truth, reason and
faith. While young people may be rebelling, they also have
a clear need for boundaries, frameworks and guidance.

You see, the new things of God are not like the
novelties of this world, all of which are temporary;
they come and go, and we keep looking for more.
The new things which God gives to our lives are
lasting, not only in the future, when we will be with
him, but today as well.[1]

We are aware that the number of church-going Catholics in
many countries is falling. This is not limited to the young and
indeed this makes the role of the school in the New Evangelisation even more important. Our school leaders now
perform a role that traditionally rested with parents in the
first instance. For many of our young people school is the
main constant in their life. It often falls to Catholic schools
and our school leaders, as the new evangelists, to be the
advocates of truth, reason and faith. The work of the Catholic
Head Teacher therefore answers the call of Pope John Paul
II that the New Evangelisation is needed where we have
people who 'have been baptised; are of good will; are perhaps
connected with us through, say, the school, but are either no
longer (or maybe are not yet) in a real, living relationship
with Christ, or have drifted from the practice of faith.'[2]

Pope Francis stated in his Apostolic Exhortation *Evangelii
Gaudium*: 'it is undeniable that many people feel disillusioned and no longer identify with the Catholic tradition.'[3]
So how do current Catholic Head Teachers reach out to
these children and young people to help them build a
relationship with Jesus Christ?

As a Catholic school leader, I always believed it was
important to provide opportunities for worship within the
school setting but I was often disappointed at participation
levels. On discussing this one day with the School Chaplain,
he offered me wise words. He suggested that we have to
continue with our ministry as this was one way of 'keeping
the pilot light lit' in the hope that one day our young
charges would find their way back to Jesus—just like the
small gas burner which is kept alight permanently to light
our central heating, boilers or cookers when needed.

In *Lumen Fidei*, Pope Francis reminds us that in John's Gospel, Christ says of himself: 'I have come as light into the world, that whoever believes in me may not remain in darkness.'[4] Saint Paul uses the same image: 'God who said "Let light shine out of darkness" has shone in our hearts.'[5]

Our school leaders work tirelessly to keep the pilot light of faith lit in the hearts and souls of the young in their care. This work manifests itself in modern school life in three main ways. Head Teachers keep the pilot lights lit by

a)   modelling their own faith;

b)   setting the tone and

c)   creating the structures to ensure that young people have opportunities to know the faith, live the faith and share the faith.

They work in this way so that young people will come to know the truth, as 'the truth will set you (them) free'.[6]

Know the Faith

Leading teaching and learning is a key function of the Head Teacher. Religious Education syllabi assist parents, teachers, catechists and clergy in their work with young people. They help us work with children and young people to do as follows:

> develop their knowledge and understanding of Catholic faith, nurture respect for other Christian traditions and world faiths, experience opportunities for spiritual growth, acquire the skills of reflection, discernment and moral decision-making and commit to beliefs, values and actions in a positive response to God's invitation to faith.[7]

The Catholic Head Teacher, as evangelist, must ensure that the rigour and professionalism teachers apply to other areas of the curriculum are also evident in the teaching and learning practised in the Religious Education classroom. We will not keep the pilot light lit if we fail to help young people know and understand the tenets of our faith and give them the skills of reflection, discernment, critical thinking and deciding how to act in accordance with an informed conscience in relation to matters of morality.[8]

Another way in which the Catholic Head Teacher promotes the New Evangelisation is by teaching on programmes of Religious Education. Primary Head Teachers are fully involved in the teaching of the Religious Education programmes in their schools and many of our secondary colleagues opt to have timetabled Religious Education classes. In most cases, this is in the senior years. We cannot underestimate how influential this work is in imparting the Word of God and in formally guiding and directing young people in their learning. Most importantly, it sends an important message across the school community as to the importance of Religious Education in the daily life of the school.

Live the Faith

The faith mission of the Catholic school is not defined only in its Religious Education programmes but in all aspects of the school's life. It is often through helping young people to live faith that we are able to assist them in knowing Christ. The Head Teacher for the New Evangelisation ensures that there are opportunities for children and young people to answer the call of the Holy Father to hear 'the cry of the earth and the cry of the poor'.[9]

The opportunities to live faith are found across all our schools. It is fitting that the New Evangelisation was supported by the declaration of the Jubilee of Mercy. The 2016 Jubilee was declared by Pope Francis in the April 2015 Papal Bull, *Misericordiae Vultus* (Latin for 'The Face of Mercy'). By framing the life of faith in the corporal works of mercy, Head Teachers are able to assist children to know and understand God.[10]

It is commonplace for schools to research, identify and give financial aid to organisations that feed the hungry both at home and overseas. Here are some examples from

Scotland, the country where I live and work. The website of the charity *Mary's Meals* carries stories of such good work. A current example is a school that raised over £8000 to help build a kitchen for a primary school in Southern Malawi to assist the community feed the children every day. In giving drink to the thirsty, we find examples of fundraising for the Scottish Catholic International Aid Fund (SCIAF) appeals such as 'Water is Life'. In Scotland, as in many other countries, classes donate money to groups, including St Vincent de Paul to provide support and services for those in need of clothing, shelter and food.

Some of our older students volunteer at soup kitchens in our large cities. They can often be seen on cold dark evenings giving of their time, energy, patience and love by assisting in the distribution of food and warm clothing to the homeless. They participate in the Big Summer Sleep Out to both understand homelessness and to raise money for The Big Issue Foundation to help make a difference.

Examples of practising the corporal work of mercy in visiting the sick and imprisoned is evidenced by the range and quality of events our schools support. Carol concerts, musical events, food parcels, Christmas dinners, Christmas gifts, coffee mornings, IT support and running the odd game of bingo are routine occurrences in many of our communities.

One may think that the Head Teacher, as evangelist, would have difficulty in providing opportunities for young people to exercise the Corporal Work of Mercy of burying the dead, however, one would be mistaken. We know that the numbers of practising Catholics in our country are falling. Therefore, in times of difficulty and in particular when dealing with the death of a close relative, it is often the Head Teacher and the school that become the focal point for families in grief. The Head Teacher supports the family and encourages pupils to do likewise. In this way, they have the opportunity to grieve and show others support during difficult times.

Many charities are supported by our schools and in turn they assist the Head Teacher in providing opportunities for children to exercise the Corporal Works of Mercy and therefore keep the pilot light lit.[11] One of the main charities our primary schools support is *Missio Scotland*. This is important as the work of *Missio* links the Corporal and the Spiritual works of mercy. It works in tandem with Catholic Primary Schools and asks children to do two things every day: pray for the children in mission areas of the world and donate a small coin. *Missio* funds help to build clinics, supply medicines and nutritional help, support education projects for children and in providing missionaries to spread the teaching of Christ.

The challenge for school leaders is to help children and young people relate to 'why' we do these things because in themselves they do not make us Catholic. Many people of all faiths (and none) are involved in charitable activities and in helping those less fortunate.

The Head Teacher's role in the New Evangelisation is to ensure that the design of school-based curricular and extra-curricular programmes have their roots in Christ. In addition, Head Teachers can use the Spiritual Works of Mercy as guide in their work. The Spiritual Works of Mercy are acts of compassion, as listed below, by which Head Teachers can help children and young people with their emotional needs and their spiritual development:

> to instruct the ignorant; to counsel the doubtful; to admonish sinners; to bear wrongs patiently; to forgive offences willingly; to comfort the afflicted and to pray for the living and the dead.

Share the Faith

In sharing the faith, the Catholic Head Teacher encourages children and young people in their faith development, provides opportunity for worship within the school and parish and in the preparation for the sacraments. However, the Head Teacher, as the new evangelist and in keeping the pilot light lit, has to model faith in order to share its power and glory.

The Head Teacher's office and indeed the school should proudly display the signs of our faith and as the leader, the Head Teacher has to be visible and active at all opportunities for worship. Being a Head Teacher in twenty-first century schools is a difficult job—indeed within the Catholic sector it must be seen as vocation. One of the many characteristics and qualities needed to be a successful school leader is undoubtedly 'patience'.

The behaviour of the Catholic Head Teacher can lead others toward Christ or drive them away.[12] The behaviours of the Head Teacher have to model Gospel values and be true to the teachings of the Church. All Gospel values begin with and derive from Jesus' love: respect for the life and dignity of each individual; trust in God; honesty; compassion; forgiveness; mercy; community; servant leadership; equality; simplicity and justice and peace.

The Catholic school leader has to be open, fair and honest in all dealings with all members of the community. They have to adhere to high standards and be very good role models due to their influence on others. They have to understand the mission they are undertaking as Catholic leaders.

Pope Francis went a stage further when addressing the leaders of the Church. He referenced fifteen 'diseases' of leadership.[13] The author of the article in *Harvard Business Review* tells us 'these diseases are a danger for every leader and every organisation, and they can strike at the individual and the community levels'. We can easily interpret the Holy Father's teaching to assist the school leader in our Catholic schools today and in turn assist them in their role as new evangelists.

In applying this teaching to school leaders, I chose to concentrate on half of these diseases and to draw up a short checklist for current holders of the post of Head Teacher. The Pope warns of the disease of thinking we are indispensable and of thinking we are better than others. The solution to this for school leaders is to remember Gospel values and that we are servant leaders. The Catholic school leader shares power, is mindful of the needs of others and helps people develop and perform as highly as possible. Servant leadership is best defined by Jesus Himself: 'Whoever wants to become great among you must be your servant, and whoever wants to be first must be your slave—just as the Son of Man did not come to be served, but to serve, and to give his life as a ransom for many.'[14]

Pope Francis warns of the disease of 'busyness'. Leaders who immerse themselves in work can neglect their own wellbeing and the wellbeing of their families. Head Teachers need to recharge their batteries and need to create time for reflection and prayer. Those who do not will find their stress levels too high and this can affect decision-making. There is no way to avoid stress when you are responsible for children, families, outcomes, and are accountable to all. The question for Head Teachers is not how to avoid stress but how best to relieve it and maintain a sense of balance. Pope Francis tells us that rest is obligatory and 'should be taken seriously: by spending time with one's family and respecting holidays as time to recharge.'

As new evangelists, Head Teachers need to avoid 'leadership Alzheimer's disease.' Unsurprisingly this consists of forgetting those who came before and assisted us by nurturing, mentoring and supporting us on our leadership journey. It is vital as a role model to acknowledge those who went before us and to understand that, as Head Teachers, we are merely passing through.

The focus of the Head Teacher on planning and preparation is to be commended but Pope Francis warns of the disease of excessive planning and of a functionalism when everything is planned down to the last detail in the belief that this will ensure success. Things need to be prepared well, but without ever falling into the temptation of trying to eliminate spontaneity and serendipity, which is always more flexible than any human planning. We need to work to avoid this disease if we are to encourage participation and inclusivity.

In our modern world, we often need to work hard to remain positive and hopeful. Head Teachers must avoid the disease of a downcast face. You see this disease in those glum and dour persons who think that to be serious you have to put on a face of melancholy and severity, and treat others — especially those we consider our inferiors — with rigour, brusqueness and arrogance. In fact, a show of severity and sterile pessimism are frequently symptoms of fear and insecurity. A leader must make an effort to be courteous, serene, enthusiastic and joyful, a person who transmits joy everywhere he goes. A happy heart radiates an infectious joy: it is immediately evident! Therefore, a leader should never lose that joyful, humorous and even self-deprecating spirit which makes people amiable even in difficult situations. How beneficial is a good dose of humour! ...[15]

The premise of this section of my reflection is that Head Teachers, by modelling Gospel values, will keep the pilot light of faith lit in the hearts of the young. In this way, they are leading for the New Evangelisation. One certain way of ensuring this does not work would be to suffer from the disease described by Pope Francis as existential schizophrenia:

> This is the disease of those who live a double life, the fruit of that hypocrisy typical of the mediocre and of a progressive emotional emptiness which no [accomplishment or] title can fill.[16]

There is a story told by a Head Teacher colleague who often reminds the teachers in the school that faith cannot be worn like an overcoat. An overcoat put on when arriving at school but discarded at the front gate on their way into the world. If we as Catholic teachers model this, then surely our young will follow suit. Leaders, especially Catholic Head Teachers cannot be hypocrites. They must always keep sight of the people they serve and 'walk the talk'.

I would always advise Head Teachers never to barricade themselves in the office surrounded by bureaucratic tasks at the expense of being with children, young people and staff during the pupil day. Sometimes this can actually spread and become the 'disease of closed circles' where the senior leadership team becomes a clique. They may start out with good intentions of providing support and challenge across the school but there is the danger that with the passing of time it creates a disconnect from pupils, staff and the wider school community.

Two of the other diseases referenced by the Holy Father are linked to power, influence and service. They are the twin diseases of rivalry and vainglory and of extravagance and self-exhibition. This is when status, benefits and titles become the driver rather than the service to communities. To be evangelists, Head Teachers must have the correct attitude and never forget their fundamental duty as leaders. Pope Francis quotes Philippians 2:3: 'Do nothing from selfishness or conceit but in humility count others better than ourselves.' As leaders for the New Evangelisation, we must look to the interests of others and not only our own interests.

The leader who turns service into power for its own sake or for selfish reasons is not modelling Gospel values and has forgotten the fundamental role of Servant Leadership. 'So let us learn how to serve, and in our lives enthrone Him; each other's needs to prefer, for it is Christ we're serving.'[17] Head Teachers leading the Catholic school for the New Evangelisation do not seek personal glory, do not seek to find ways to show that they are more capable than others, do not slander or discredit others and do not put themselves on display to gain personal plaudits.[18]

Evaluating the Work of the Catholic School.

We have a strong and successful culture of self-evaluation in schools and education leaders are comfortable with self-evaluation tools. Effective self-evaluation is the starting point for all school improvement. A set of indicators help Head Teachers and teachers in school self-evaluation and also assist education authorities and national inspectorate in discharging their responsibilities for quality assurance. In Scotland, for example, a nationally agreed and accepted set of quality indicators for school self-evaluation also provide opportunities for partnerships at all levels of the education system. Since 1996, *How Good is our School?* has become a nationally and internationally recognised brand, which underpins effective self-evaluation as the starting point for school improvement. *How Good is our School?* provides a suite of quality indicators that support staff in all sectors to look inwards, to scrutinise their work and evaluate what is working well for learners and what could be better. It is a key aspect of the Scottish approach to school improvement. The framework is designed to be used to support self-evaluation and reflection by practitioners at all levels.[19]

Self-evaluation frameworks and quality indicators provide parameters and priorities while taking advantage of local flexibilities. When used well and appropriately, these self-evaluation tools and the professional dialogue they engender lead to real improvement which benefits children and young people in our schools. If they are only used for external quality assurance they serve a lesser purpose and have little impact on lasting improved per-formance or increased outcomes for children and young people. The set of quality indicators can provide a 'health check' for schools and help identify where improvement should be focussed.

Maybe it would be useful therefore to share this potential checklist, adapted from *Harvard Business Review* article of April 2015, to assist Head Teachers in gauging their current state of health.

How Good Are You at Avoiding the Diseases of Leadership

Example: if you feel you have a very good work–life balance and therefore do not suffer from disease of 'busyness' you would tick 5 or 6 for Question Two.

		1	2	3	4	5	6
1	I consider myself a servant leader						
2	I demonstrate a healthy work-life balance						
3	I use intuition and improvisation rather than over relying on plans						
4	I recognise the debt I owe to those who supported and mentored me?						
5	I set little store by the rewards and privileges of headship						
6	I fully engage with pupils and staff in the life and work of the school						
7	I recognise and celebrate the motives and accomplishments of others						
8	I cultivate a fun and joy-filled work environment						
9	I am selfless when it comes to sharing rewards and praise						

KEY

LEVEL 6: excellent outstanding
LEVEL 5: very good, major strengths
LEVEL 4: good important strengths with areas for improvement
LEVEL 3: satisfactory—strengths just outweigh weaknesses
LEVEL 2: weak important weaknesses
LEVEL 1: unsatisfactory, major weaknesses.

If Head Teachers wish to use this health check, it would be more valid if they seek evidence to support—or indeed refute—the evaluations. Triangulation is the process commonly used in education to ensure that the evaluative statements are grounded in a robust evidence base. Such triangulation should include data and involve all school staff, learners, partners and other stakeholders. Thus, brave leaders could seek staff, pupil and parental views and ask a colleague to observe their practice.

Knowing, Living and Sharing Faith in Catholic Schools

Current Catholic Head Teachers know and understand that many people, including the young, feel disillusioned and no longer identify with the Catholic tradition. They have to help young people make sense of their world and how this relates to the teachings of Christ. Therefore, their role is to exemplify and create opportunities of faith in action to 'keep the pilot light lit' and assist people to build a relationship with Jesus now or in the future.

An excellent example of linking knowing the Faith, living the Faith and sharing Faith are two initiatives from Scotland: the *Pope Benedict XVI Caritas Award* and *Pope Francis Faith Award*. Secondary Head Teachers embraced the *Caritas Award* when it was introduced in 2011. Large numbers of pupils were enrolled in year one and this has continued to grow since. This young person's award scheme focuses on three areas: Faith Witness, Faith Learning and Faith Reflection. Over one school session, senior pupils volunteer within their communities to share the gifts God gave them for the good of others. These volunteering activities include leading the Children's Liturgy, visiting the sick and helping in the charity shop. Participants must also produce a personal journal detailing their growth and faith journey during the time spent on the programme.

Following the success of this approach, the scheme was extended and we saw the birth of the *Pope Francis Faith Award*. This programme is designed to help our Primary 6 and Primary 7 (aged 10–11) children use the gifts of the Holy Spirit to have positive impact on their class, school and home. It provides an opportunity for them to act out the words of Pope Francis when he said to young people at Easter in 2013:

> How beautiful it would be if each of you, every evening, could say: 'Today at school, at home, at work, guided by God, I showed a sign of love towards one of my friends, my parents, an older person!'[20]

Knowing, Living and Sharing Faith in Secular Settings

Those who are Catholic and teach and lead within a faith school are indeed fortunate. While there are trials and tribulations as a Head Teacher working for the New Evangelisation within our Catholic schools, it is important to pause and consider how more challenging this must be in a secular setting.

Catholics working in any school as the Head Teacher can still perform their duty as a teacher and as a Christian to help to give pupils values that they could live by throughout their lives. Pupils can easily lose sight of what really matters because we are living in an increasingly secular and materialistic society.

Across education systems, including those in the United Kingdom, vision statements and curriculum emphasise values for all schools. In Scotland, *Curriculum for Excellence* is based on a set of values. The values of wisdom, justice, compassion and integrity are the words which are inscribed on the mace of the Scottish Parliament. They are also the values to underpin policies, practice and the curriculum itself. Therefore, it is entirely permissible and indeed desirable for Christians to help to instil good morals and values such as tolerance and compassion.

In a recent speech to Catholic leaders in England, Sir Michael Wilshaw, until recently Ofsted's Chief Inspector said that it has never been more important for Christians to stand up for their faith:

> The parable of the Prodigal Son was always my
> touchstone for the way I dealt with difficult situa-
> tions and intransigent youngsters. As a Head
> Teacher, nothing gave me more joy and satisfaction
> than seeing someone who had started out badly, and
> been written off, coming right in the end.[21]

Within most self-evaluation toolkits and inspection regimes,
schools and those who teach and lead them are expected to
demonstrate passionate commitment to ensuring social justice, children's rights, learning for sustainability and equality
as important prerequisites for all involved in education.

The themes of leadership, partnership, shared values,
wellbeing, social justice and equality are the foundation
stones of an excellent school and, as such, need to be firmly
embedded within self-evaluation.[22]

Ofsted is also actively inspecting how well schools are
promoting values such as tolerance and respect. Advice to
those who are working in secular settings differs little from
that set out in this chapter:

- model your own faith and values;

- set the tone of your school to match gospel values
  of wisdom, justice, compassion and integrity;

- help young people make sense of their world;

- create structures to ensure that young people have
  opportunities to serve and work with those less
  fortunate;

- recharge your batteries and create time for reflection and prayer.

Concluding remarks

In society today we are familiar with the motif of 'Five a
day', mostly expressed in terms of the health benefits of
eating fresh fruit and vegetables. In early education we
embrace the 'Five to Thrive' approach to attachment and
attunement as processes that forge bonds between young

children and their parents and or carers. At the heart of 'five to thrive' are the key activities for parents of Respond; Cuddle; Relax; Play and Talk when dealing with very young children. These are regarded as the building blocks of positive interaction and happy, healthy children.

So as leaders for the New Evangelisation what could our 'five to thrive' for Catholic Head Teachers be? What would be our building blocks to ensure positive interaction between children and school leaders that could in turn build positive relationships with Jesus? What five recommendations would we make to assist the Head Teacher in the New Evangelisation with young people who are connected with us through, say, the school, but are either no longer (or maybe are not yet) in a real, living relationship with Christ, or have drifted from the practice of faith?[23]

The 'five to thrive' for Head Teachers would be: patience; love; providing opportunities for young people to live the Corporal Works of Mercy; providing opportunities for young people to exercise the Spiritual Works of Mercy and teach by your example.[24] By this approach Head Teachers will keep the pilot light of faith lit in the hearts and souls of the young in the hope that in answering the following question, set them by Pope Benedict, their answers will be a Catholic school leader and teacher:

> We live in a celebrity culture, and young people are often encouraged to model themselves on figures from the world of sport or entertainment. My question for you is this: what are the qualities you see in others that you would most like to have yourselves? What kind of person would you really like to be? [25]

Head Teachers working for the New Evangelisation have the opportunity to put into practice their mission. In the words of John Henry Cardinal Newman:

> God has created me to do Him some definite service. He has committed some work to me which He has not committed to another.

This definite service will include keeping the pilot light of faith lit in the hearts of our children and young people in the hope that they will develop meaningful relationships with Christ. In announcing the Holy Year of Mercy, Pope Francis reminded us that we, by being merciful, will 'live in the light of the word of the Lord'.

The theme of 'light' has been the golden thread running through this reflection on the role of the Head Teacher in the New Evangelisation. In conclusion, it seems fitting to end with a prayer by John Henry Cardinal Newman, not only because it emphasises the mission of the evangelist but because I served as Head Teacher of the only school in Scotland with Newman as its patron. It is a great strength to serve in a Catholic school when one has access to the rich words and writing of such a father of the Church who is also the patron. No school assembly, Mass or other service was complete without 'Praise to the Holiest' or 'Lead Kindly Light' being sung.

The following Newman radiance prayer has been adapted and used across the world for many years. It was the daily prayer recited by Mother Teresa and her Sisters working in the poor communities of India.

Dear Jesus, help me to spread Your fragrance everywhere I go.
Flood my soul with Your spirit and life.
Penetrate and possess my whole being so utterly,
That my life may only be a radiance of Yours.

Shine through me, and be so in me
That every soul I come in contact with
May feel Your presence in my soul.
Let them look up and see no longer me, but only Jesus!

Stay with me and then I shall begin to shine as You shine,
So to shine as to be a light to others;
The light, O Jesus will be all from You; none of it will be mine;
It will be you, shining on others through me.

Let me thus praise You the way You love best, by shining
on those around me.
Let me preach You without preaching, not by words but
by my example,
By the catching force of the sympathetic influence of what
I do,
The evident fullness of the love my heart bears to You.
Amen.

The Head Teacher, in leading the Catholic School for the
New Evangelisation, will find both support and challenge
in this prayer, calling on our Lord to help others to see Him
in their words, in their actions and in how they live their
lives.

Notes

1   *Pope Francis*. Homily, 28 April 2013.
2   Pope John Paul II, *Redemptoris Missio*.
3   Pope Francis, *Evangelii Gaudium*.
4   John 12:46.
5   2 Corinthians 4:6.
6   John 8:32.
7   SCES http://sces.org.uk/this-is-our-faith.
8   *Catechism of the Catholic Church*, 1992, 1783–1785.
9   Pope Francis, *Laudato Si'*.
10   The Corporal Works of Mercy are found in the teachings of Jesus
     and give us a model for how we should treat all others, as if they
     were Christ in disguise. See CCC 2447: 'The *works of mercy* are
     charitable actions by which we come to the aid of our neighbour in
     his spiritual and bodily necessities. Instructing, advising, consoling,
     comforting are spiritual works of mercy, as are forgiving and bearing
     wrongs patiently. The corporal works of mercy consist especially in
     feeding the hungry, sheltering the homeless, clothing the naked,
     visiting the sick and imprisoned, and burying the dead. Among all
     these, giving alms to the poor is one of the chief witnesses to fraternal
     charity: it is also a work of justice pleasing to God.'
11   These charities include Hosanna House and Children's Pilgrimage
     Trust (HCPT); Let the Children Live; Marie Curie Cancer Care; Aid
     to Church in Need; Society for the Protection of Unborn Children

(SPUC); the various hospices and organisations specifically working to help children with health issues.

[12] 'Everyone should be quick to listen, slow to speak and slow to become angry, for man's anger does not bring about the righteous life that God desires.' (James 1:19–2).

[13] G. Hamel, 'The 15 Diseases of Leadership, according to Pope Francis' in *Harvard Business Review*. 14 April 2015.

[14] Matthew 20:26–28.

[15] 'A miserable heart means a miserable life; a cheerful heart fills the day with song".' (Proverbs 15:15).

[16] Hamel, 'The 15 Diseases of Leadership, according to Pope Francis'.

[17] Jesus told His disciples, 'If anyone would come after Me, let him deny himself and take up his cross and follow Me' (Matthew 16:24). This is also beautifully captured in the hymn Our Servant King when we sing: "So let us learn how to serve, and in our lives enthrone Him; each other's needs to prefer, for it is Christ we're serving" (G. Kendrick, 1983 Thankyou Music).

[18] 'If anyone wants to boast, let him boast of the Lord' (1 Corinthians 1:31).

[19] Education Scotland, *How Good is our School* 4th Edition (2015). Available at: http://www.educationscotland.gov.uk/resources /h/hgios4/introduction.asp.

[20] *Pope Francis, Homily*, 28 April 2013.

[21] M. Wilshaw, *Times Educational Supplement* (29 January 2016).

[22] Education Scotland, *How Good is our School?*

[23] Pope John Paul II, *Redemptoris Missio*.

[24] 'I call you friends says the Lord because I have made known to you everything I have learned from my Father' (John 15:15).

[25] Pope Benedict XVI, *Address at St Mary's University College, Twickenham*, 17 September 2010.

THE SCHOOL CHAPLAIN AND THE NEW EVANGELISATION

*But they will not ask his help unless they believe in
him, and they will not believe in him unless they
have heard of him, and they will not hear of him
unless they get a preacher, and they will not have a
preacher unless one is sent, but as scripture says:
The footsteps of those who bring good news is a
welcome sound.*

Romans 10:14–15.

I N THE TWO millennia since St Paul wrote these words,
since his were those footsteps bringing the welcome
sound of the Gospel, the Church has been untiring in
her missionary work. Many are the people throughout
history who have followed in St Paul's footsteps and varied
are the forms of evangelisation they engaged in. In the
Foreword to the companion volume to this book, *Reclaiming
the Piazza: Catholic Education as a Cultural Project*, Archbishop
Philip Tartaglia of Glasgow writes:

> The challenge of how best to transmit the life-giving
> message of the Gospel is one that has accompanied
> Christians down through the ages since Christ's
> command, 'Euntes Docete' (go, teach) was first
> heard by the Apostles. Over the millennia, the
> Catholic Church has combined fidelity to the deposit
> of faith bequeathed by Christ, with creative and
> ever-new methods of proclamation, engagement and
> dialogue. In our own era we have had to come to
> terms with a dramatic re-alignment in the relation-
> ship between Church and wider society. In a very
> short time the Christian message has gone from

being the bedrock of our culture to becoming the
most counter-cultural message of the age.[1]

The Church is by her very nature missionary and so will
always engage in evangelisation, but Archbishop Tartaglia
points to the need for what St John Paul II called the New
Evangelisation, a multi-faceted reality that includes a
're-evangelisation' of those societies that have moved away
from their Christian roots.

Catholic schools have perhaps been one of the most
fruitful methods the Church has found in response to
Christ's command and have served the Church throughout
the world, in supporting parents in forming their children
in the faith. Indeed, the Congregation for Catholic Education in the document *The Religious Dimension of Education in
a Catholic School* recognises their importance to the life of
the Catholic community:

> The church gradually develops its pastoral instru-
> ments so that they become ever more effective in
> proclaiming the Gospel and promoting total human
> formation. The Catholic school is one of these instru-
> ments ... [It] has had a clear identity, not only as a
> presence of the church in society, but also as a
> genuine and proper instrument of the church. It is a
> place of evangelization, of authentic apostolate and
> of pastoral action.[2]

The Catholic school serves the Church in a twofold way:
first, as a place where the sound of the Good News rings
out, and second, as a community of those who have
welcomed that sound, a faith community, 'a place of
ecclesial experience'.[3] These two will come together in the
lives of many students (and perhaps staff) for whom the
Catholic school is their only experience of the world of faith:
baptised as infants and having received the other Sacraments of Initiation, they have no real experience of the
'domestic Church' nor of the local parish community. The
community of faith that is the Catholic school is for some
Catholics their only contact with the Church into which they

have been baptised, for others it is an extension of their parish and home faith communities, and for others it is an encounter with the Church serving the world beyond her own borders.

The effectiveness of the school as a Gospel-inspired community and as an instrument of evangelisation, will very much depend on the work of those within, staff and students, including the school Chaplain. He is one of the 'preachers' sent that others may hear and respond to the Gospel and so come to live it in the midst of the community that is the Church. This chapter will explore the role of the Chaplain in the Catholic school, indicating how his ministry must be firmly rooted in the Faith that the New Evangelisation invites people to welcome.

The School Chaplain: Developing the Four Catechetical Pillars

Appreciating the Catholic school as an 'experience of the Church' provides a context in which to understand the role of the Chaplain.[4] His ministry is grounded in the missionary and pastoral work of the Church; it is centred on the school as a community of faith. To understand the place of the Chaplain in a school it is essential to understand what a community of faith looks like and how it can be realised within an educational institution. A full exposition of this is beyond the scope of the chapter but a brief description will illustrate possible avenues for the work of the Chaplain.

St Peter's inspiring words on the day of Pentecost led to the conversion of many Israelites: 'That very day about three thousand were added to their number.'[5] St Luke continues, telling us that, 'These remained faithful to the teaching of the apostles, to the brotherhood, to the breaking of bread and to the prayers.'[6] These four dimensions are central to the life of faith, to the life of the faith community, and naturally make their way into the *Catechism of the Catholic Church* as it offers 'an *organic presentation* of the Catholic faith in its entirety'.[7] The *Catechism* clearly states that the unity of the faith is rooted in the mystery of the unity of the One God who is a Trinity of Persons, but presents the Faith of the Church under four distinct though interconnected pillars:

- The Profession of Faith;

- The Sacraments of Faith;

- The Life of Faith;

- Prayer in the Life of Faith.

St John Paul II when presenting the *Catechism* to the world, highlights the unity of these four aspects:

> The confession of faith finds its proper place in the celebration of worship. Grace, the fruit of the sacraments, is the irreplaceable condition for Christian living, just as participation in the Church's liturgy requires faith. If faith is not expressed in works, it is dead (cf. Jas 2:14–16) and cannot bear fruit unto eternal life.[8]

Faith, lived within the Church, involves: a Faith that is held in common—a unifying and identifying belief system; an encounter with the mystery of God in the sacramental and liturgical celebration of the faith; the living of the Faith in the grace-filled life of charity and, in the life of prayer, the 'speaking of heart to heart' in intimate dialogue. The revelation of God and the response of faith takes place in the life of the Church through the dynamic interaction of these four aspects, which must be present in the life of the community and in the spiritual journey of the individual believer.

Each particular community of faith is called to manifest the fullness of the life of faith and so will realise the four dimensions in the concrete situation, including the educational context of the school. These four facets give a theological grounding to the work of the Chaplain in a Catholic school but can also provide the basis of a framework in which to plan, organise and evaluate his work; they ensure that the Chaplain stays grounded in a faith-based ministry in the midst of all the different roles he will take on and as the activities he becomes involved in multiply. Planning and reviewing his ministry in the light of these four pillars will also ensure that his ministry is a balanced one, not weighted towards the liturgical and sacramental at the expense of the pastoral, or overly directed towards social justice while neglecting prayer.

The Faith Professed

Faith is first of all a response, the entrusting of self to the God who graciously reveals Himself to us. In so doing, He reveals also our divine origin and destiny as well as His plan for our salvation. The Catholic Faith is a revealed faith. That revelation is mediated through the Church, including the professions of faith that are the creedal statements of the Church.[9] The content of God's self-revelation, the *Depositum Fidei*, is expressed in the doctrinal teachings of the Church and the act of faith by the believer includes an assent to them.

The giving of assent requires a knowledge of what is being assented to and so the life of faith necessarily involves an initial and ongoing doctrinal formation, a deepening of the believer's knowledge and comprehension of the Catholic faith. This is not for purely academic purposes but rather to facilitate an ever-deepening entry into the mystery of God which brings a more profound communion with him, and a stronger unity with the community which professes the same Faith.

The ministry of the Chaplain will include the shared profession of faith. This will involve the communal recitation of the Creed in Holy Mass and other liturgical contexts, but will also involve him in leading others to know and understand the revealed Faith. The Chaplain will, within the boundaries of his ministry, be a teacher of the Faith; this is an integral part of his ministry: the sanctifying, governing and teaching ministry of the bishop in which he shares.

While it is unlikely that a Chaplain will be a qualified teacher, it is reasonable to expect that he will have a theological competency and pedagogical ability that can be put at the service of the teaching of the Faith. While he might not be a member of a team of qualified specialist teachers of Religious Education, it is natural that there will be a close affinity between the duties of the Chaplain and the work of those charged with leading the school in Religious Education.[10] The Chaplain may find himself, therefore, involved in working with Religious Education teachers in the preparation of resources, in presenting specific aspects of the faith as an 'expert speaker', in supporting the catechetical dimension of the subject through leading prayer and retreat experiences that supplement the work in the classroom. He will work especially closely with teachers who are preparing children to receive the Sacraments. These points of contact will benefit the work of the Chaplain as well as the Religious Education Department by offering structured activities through which the Chaplain can interact with students, supporting their faith development and offering the witness of his own faith.

The teaching ministry of the Chaplain is not restricted to students and can be exercised in supporting the faith development of staff. A myriad of activities can be conceived of here, from Bible Study Groups, faith sharing opportunities, input on the nature and mission of Catholic education at staff in-service days, presentations on different aspects of the faith, etc. Again, a close link with the Religious Education Department suggests itself as the Chaplain may be able to support teachers to understand the particular aspects of scripture and doctrine that they will be involved in teaching. For example, the Chaplain may host a tutorial with staff as they prepare to teach a unit of work, giving some theological and scriptural background and answering any questions that may arise.

It is worth reiterating that despite the potential to contribute to the teaching of Religious Education, the

Chaplain's role cannot be limited to supporting the work of the Religious Education Department. His ministry should be recognised as pertaining to and permeating the whole school. The faith life of the school is not the sole preserve and responsibility of the Religious Education Department and the work of the Chaplain should not be reduced to a part of its remit. The other dimensions of his faith ministry should ensure that this does not happen, such as the liturgical life of the school.

The Faith Celebrated

St John Paul II echoed the Second Vatican Council's presentation of the Eucharist as the high point of the life of the Church when he said that 'The Church draws her life from the Eucharist.'[11] In the Eucharist is found the origin of the Church, the celebration and making present of her central mystery—the Paschal event—and the source of her life. In the celebration of Holy Mass, the Church is most visibly who she truly is: the Spirit-filled assembly of those redeemed by the Son, united with the heavenly choirs, giving praise through Him to the Father. The intimate connection between the Eucharist and the Church is expressed in the *Catechism* thus:

> As the work of Christ liturgy is also an action of his *Church*. It makes the Church present and manifests her as the visible sign of the communion in Christ between God and men. It engages the faithful in the new life of the community and involves the 'conscious, active and fruitful participation' of everyone.[12]

This can be no less true of the 'scholastic Church'. Everything that happens in the Catholic school should flow from and lead to the celebration of the Eucharist. The Chaplain will obviously find here an important locus for his ministry. (This is no less true of lay chaplains who will take on the responsibility of facilitating the celebration of Holy Mass by inviting priests to the school.)

The life of the Catholic school throughout the year is marked by many occasions when the celebration of Holy Mass will be fitting: the beginning of a new year, its drawing to a close at summer, the Patronal Feast Day, the highpoints of the Liturgical Calendar, not least the Holidays of Obligation, exams, etc. The Chaplain may also find himself celebrating Holy Mass for particular or extraordinary moments in the life of the school community: in response to an immediate need or situations such as staff or student illness, a death, a retirement, a staff retreat or in-service day, and where possible on a more frequent basis as part of the weekly school programme either before the day begins or at lunchtime.

The Eucharist can also be central to the life of the school though periods of Exposition of the Blessed Sacrament, either as part of an organised programme or on a voluntary basis during lunchtime or interval. The encounter with Christ in the Blessed Sacrament is currently an important part of Youth Ministry due to events such as Night Fever and Youth 2000 and the opportunity for this in schools will support this development of a Eucharistic spirituality.

Celebrating the Sacrament of Reconciliation is invaluable to the life and growth of the school as a community of faith. These precious experiences of pardon and mercy can allow personal and communal healing and witness to the values of compassion and forgiveness that underpin the ethos of the school. It can offer spiritual depth to an Advent or Lenten programme and often provides an opportunity that might otherwise not have been possible.

The Chaplain may find himself involved in the celebration of other Sacraments on an ad hoc basis. The school, as previously noted, may be the only faith community a student knows and may be the place where he/she responds to God's invitation to faith, involving the Chaplain in the RCIA process. A member of staff, or a previous student, may invite the Chaplain to be part of their own particular faith journey by celebrating their wedding, the baptism of their child, etc. These remind the Chaplain of the school's connection with the local Church and his work will be an important point of contact between the school and the parish or parishes that its students come from. The attendance of primary school pupils at 'First Friday Mass' is one example of a celebration enjoyed by parishioners and pupils alike, emphasising the school's integral relationship with the local faith community.

The Faith Lived

St James reminded the early disciples that: 'Faith is like that: if good works do not go with it, it is quite dead.'[13] Where the first two pillars of the Catechism concern the activity of God, the second half of the Catechism speaks of man's response. Enlivened by the Holy Spirit, the disciple lives as a child of God and calls on his 'Abba, Father' in prayer.

That the ethos of Catholic schools is often commented on is evidence of the faith lived within the school. Beyond the visible expressions familiar to Catholicism, this lies in the relationships that are encouraged and fostered among staff and students. The dignity of the individual as a child of God, made in His image and likeness, is upheld as the basis for relationships at all levels. Members of the school community are called on to grow ever closer to Christ and in His likeness through obedience to His commandment to love their neighbour. Charitable work is an essential feature of the faith community, both in supporting those in need within the community and reaching out to the world beyond the school.

The Chaplain will find no end of possibilities for his ministry in this field. Perhaps the most important is the witness of his own life. The work of the Chaplain must be modelled on the Good Shepherd who laid down His life for his sheep; his ministry should be seen as one of service and be exercised in a way that exhibits the virtues that are inspired by the Gospel. The Chaplain will model relationships that are loving, compassionate, forgiving, accepting, and encouraging. He will be involved in, and perhaps the driving force behind, projects that seek to benefit others, such as initiatives to help those in the local area or in response to more global needs, responding to ongoing situations or to one-off events.

The energy and goodwill of young people when faced with the sufferings of others is inspirational and can be a focus for the work of the Chaplain. There will be no shortage of charitable initiatives that the Chaplain can participate in or lead. His involvement will be a continual reminder that the life of the school, and the charitable works it engages in, are based on the love of God and not simply doing good for the sake of doing good. They are the signs of the Kingdom present and at work in the world, they are testimony to God's presence and an opportunity for students to embody the transformative love of God, seeking to make God present to others through their actions.

This opens up a further dimension to the work of the Chaplain—that of discernment. The Chaplain may be called upon to help direct the impulse to charity into projects that are truly positive, reminding the school community that not every charitable organisation furthers the good of the individual and society, and that many charities promote values that contradict a Christian morality and sponsor a vision of the human person that is in opposition to a Christian anthropology. In this sense the Chaplain is a prophet in the school: he calls the community to examine all that it does in the light of the Gospel.

Diane Tragele, speaking of the 'Chaplain as Prophet', said:

> Chaplains may be allowed to exercise a prophetic voice and to point to benchmarks against which the values and practices of every area of school life can be measured. These may include its ethos, policy documents and expectations of behaviour from both staff and pupils and a Christian approach to 'failure'. In a setting which is measured by achievement and results, sharing the limitless and abundant grace and love of

God, and facilitating dialogue between these ideals, could be a key factor in the ministry of chaplaincy.[14]

The Chaplain will clearly work with those in positions of leadership within the school to help promote and ensure that the Catholicity of the school is not simply skin deep but truly embedded in the heart of the school, giving life to everything that happens there. However, especially in the case of a priest (or religious where the functions of the Chaplain have been entrusted to a Brother or Sister), often his mere presence, especially when clearly identifiable through his distinctive dress, is witness and reminder enough of the nature of the school as a faith community, a testimony to the choices made at all levels about the identity and mission of the school. The Chaplain witnesses not only to his own faith, but the faith of the whole community.

The Faith Prayed

Faithful to the Apostolic teaching, nourished at the 'breaking of bread' and the life of charity, the early disciples also cultivated their faith by prayer. The God who revealed Himself in the Incarnation of the Son, calls them as a community and as individuals into a living relationship with Him. "In the New Covenant, prayer is the living relationship of the children of God with their Father who is good beyond measure, with his Son Jesus Christ and with the Holy Spirit."[15] The tradition from which the original disciples came offered a treasure from which the prayer of the community could draw, especially the Psalms and other sacred texts, and was given new life in the Prayer of the Lord.

The Chaplain in a Catholic school will call the community to prayer, supporting individuals and groups to grow in their relationship with God through an active prayer life. In what may be seen as an extension of his prophetic role he will remind the school community and each of its members of the need to ground the life of the school in prayer and to return everything to the Father in prayer. This opens various avenues to his ministry, from presiding at

communal prayer moments, to spiritual direction, to training others to be leaders in prayer.

The prayer life of the school cannot rest solely on the
shoulders of the Chaplain if it is to permeate every aspect
of school life; he will require that others take on the
responsibility of leading prayer. This may be the teacher
beginning the day/lesson with a prayer, or it may be
students leading an assembly. Whatever the form, the
Chaplain will be able to assist in the provision of resources,
in explaining different forms of prayer and by teaching
others how to lead people in prayer.

The Chaplain will, of course, lead the community in
prayer himself. While many resources exist that are directly
related to school life, he will also find a rich vein of activity
in the devotional life of the Church, in her treasury of
prayers and blessings. The many forms of devotion to the
saints, especially to the Blessed Virgin Mary, can find a
home in the school; Advent and Lenten traditions such as
the Stations of the Cross, prayers for the Holy Souls during
November. These and many other Catholic traditions can
help keep the ecclesial identity of the school alive while
nourishing individuals on their spiritual journey.

The Chaplain may be sought out to guide students or
members of staff in their prayer life through Spiritual
Direction. This can result from a desire to delve deeper into
the spiritual life or it can come about in reaction to a
particular event in that person's life. The Chaplain can help
a person come to see where God is at work in their life and
how to respond to Him. It is here that a link with the
Pastoral Care Team can be situated. The Chaplain will
naturally have a concern for the wellbeing of those in his
care and so will work closely with Pastoral Care teachers,
especially when a student, or member of staff, is experienc-
ing a difficulty. The Pastoral Care Team will be able to draw
on a variety of agencies to help, such as psychological
services, family support groups, etc. While the Chaplain
himself may have a counselling qualification and able to

serve in this role, the unique contribution he brings is the opportunity to explore the particular situation in the light of the Gospel, contextualising it within the person's relationship with God and helping them to see God present even in the midst of hardship or suffering.

The School Chaplain: the Footsteps of One who Brings Good News

David O'Malley speaks of the school Chaplain as one who represents and reveals the presence of Christ in the community. He is 'required to be the Good News for the individual or group with whom they are working'[16] and in being so he stands in a great tradition of those who, beginning with the Twelve Apostles, heard the Lord's command 'Euntes docete', and went forth to preach the Gospel. The Chaplain in the Catholic school gives witness to what Pope Francis reminds us is the 'joy of the Gospel' and so draws others to join with him in professing and celebrating the mysteries of the Faith and in responding to God's call in the life of charity and prayer. His ministry is part of the evangelising and pastoral ministry of the Church; he stands as witness to the Gospel and supports the school in offering to staff and students an experience of the Church, an extension of the Church to which they belong, or a witness to Christian life for others. As contemporary society moves further and further from the dry land that is its Christian heritage, the role of the school, and so of the Chaplain, takes on a greater importance and urgency; in a world where the welcome sound of the Gospel is being drowned out, the New Evangelisation will find in Catholic schools, in its students, staff and Chaplains, the community of disciples who remain faithful to the Apostles, to the brotherhood and to the breaking of bread, and to the prayers, those who preach what they have heard, who speak of what they know, celebrate, live and pray, those who speak of what they have seen, 'the Word, who is life'.[17]

Notes

1   R. Convery, L. Franchi and R. McCluskey, *Reclaiming the Piazza*: *Catholic Education as a Cultural Project* (Gracewing, Leominster, 2014), p. xi.

2   Congregation for Catholic Education, *The Religious Dimension of Education in a Catholic School*, 1988, 31–33.

3   Congregation for Catholic Education, *The Catholic School on the Threshold of the Third Millennium*, 1997, 12.

4   The term Chaplain will be used throughout this chapter with specific reference to a priest, in accordance with the understanding of the term as found in Canon 564 of *The Code of Canon Law*, but the reader should keep in mind that in the concrete situation the duties associated with the Chaplain are sometimes entrusted to a lay person, a religious brother or sister, or a chaplaincy team.

5   Acts 2:41.

6   Acts 2:42.

7   CCC 18.

8   Pope John Paul II, Apostolic Constitution *Fidei Depositum* (1992).

9   The two used in the Sacred Liturgy being the Nicene Creed and the Apostles Creed. It is important to remember though: 'We do not believe in formulae, but in those realities they express, which faith allows us to touch' (CCC 170).

10 'Each has a part to play in the twin tasks of religious education and the faith formation of pupils.' Scottish Catholic Education Service, *Chaplaincy in Catholic Secondary Schools in Scotland* (2009), 4.5.1.

11 Pope St John Paul II, *Ecclesia de Eucharistia* (2003) 1.

12 CCC 1071.

13 James 2:14.

14 D. Tregale, *Fresh Experiences of School Chaplaincy* (Cambridge: Grove Books Limited, 2011), p. 8.

15 CCC 2565.

16 D. O'Malley SDB, *School Ethos and Chaplaincy* (Bolton: Don Bosco Publications, 2008), p. 60.

17 1 John 1:1.

THE RELIGIOUS EDUCATION TEACHER: MAKING THE NEW EVANGELISATION HAPPEN

Natalie Finnigan

TTACHING THE WORD 'new' to anything invariably risks that particular thing becoming dated and irrelevant as time passes. It is appropriate, however, that the New Evangelisation, as described by Saint John Paul II and developed by Pope Emeritus Benedict XVI, remains just that—new. Prevailing cultural influences and social and political structures are always in motion and so too the Church's response to these must always be new. If the Church's fundamental identity is to be found in evangelisation, then the 'New Evangelisation' sees the re-articulation of this mission in light of a 'growing indifference to God', particularly within cultures which would traditionally have been Christian, whilst utilising every available resource to realign all evangelising efforts with the person of Jesus Christ.[1]

Of course, the responsibility of every Christian is to 'proclaim Christ to all people' but we know that within the community of the Church and within a variety of situations there can be any number of ways in which this can be realised.[2] Catholic teachers (whether fully conscious of this reality or not) make up the largest group currently contributing to this mission, or put another way, the largest group with the potential to contribute to this mission. In addition to this, I would suggest that making the New Evangelisation happen within an educational setting extends far beyond those for whom Religious Education (RE) is a specialist subject; it extends to those charged with teaching RE in addition to their own particular subject. It is something that necessarily involves anyone in any position who is contributing to realising the demands of Christian edu-

cation in our Catholic schools. From parents as first educators, to support staff, classroom teachers, outside agencies,
kitchen staff and management: all have a vital role to play
in this endeavour and intrinsic to all of this is the relationship of the school with the institutional Church. Only within
this comprehensive understanding of the nature of the
Church does the distinctive identity of the Catholic school
and its existence in service of the Gospel make any sense.

The focus for this particular chapter will be upon the role
of the RE teacher in making the New Evangelisation
happen. I will examine this particular vocation as understood within the wider context of the educational aims of
Christian education, distinct from other educational establishments and as part of the mission of the whole Church.
This examination will take into account the principles that
guide our understanding of the unique identity of Catholic
educational institutions, our mandate as such, and our
responsibilities both as RE teachers and as a Church.

Where Do We Want To Be?

As educators we are fluent in the language of educational
aims, learning intentions and experiences and outcomes.
Perhaps, then, it would be fruitful to ask what the aims of
the New Evangelisation are within the context of schools.
By the time students have completed their Catholic school
career, what would we expect them to have gained? And
how can RE teachers facilitate this process? Professor Tracey
Rowland reflects on this same question:

> ... after some twelve years in a Catholic educational
> system, one needs to be able to say that one's
> graduates have Catholic intellects, Catholic wills,
> Catholic imaginations and Catholic memories all
> working in tandem together and brought into a
> coherent symphony by a Catholic heart.[3]

The breadth of this challenge is massive and, of course, is
not the sole responsibility of the RE teacher. The success of

this endeavour also relies upon parents fulfilling their duties as first educators all set within a context of a functioning and functional relationship with the wider Church as an indispensable partner in this tripartite relationship.

Just as a good teacher will share with students what they are learning and how they will know they have learned it in any given lesson or unit of work, so we too as dynamic agents of the Church's mission need to make sure that we are all aware of what it is we are communally aiming for and how to best achieve it whilst also recognising our own distinct role within this project as RE teachers. This requires a strong sense of identity and purpose at all levels. Our identity as Catholic schools is not separate from the identity of the Church; rather, all missionary actions exist in harmony to serve the overriding project of human formation.

If those qualities Professor Rowland describes are what we hope to make incarnate in Catholic schools, then all involved in this ambitious endeavour must know and believe in what is distinct about Catholic education. Parents should understand the choice they make when they decide to send their children to a Catholic school and do everything in their power to support and enhance their child's faith development in tandem with their academic development. Teachers (and formators of teachers) should have a personal faith and a knowledge of Church teaching that is never static but which constantly grows and develops; and the Church should always seek new and inventive ways in which to engage staff and students in our educational institutions to take part in the New Evangelisation. As a Church the success of this project relies upon all partners realising, and positively responding to, the challenge that lies before them.

Ideally, Catholic students within our schools will be active members of their own parishes. And although in reality this might not be the case, challenges that arise from lack of contact with parishes, whilst being far from ideal, give rise to any number of opportunities that may allow the RE teacher to become a mediator between students and their families and the parish, with the ability to re-open or establish new lines of communication and, therefore, facilitate contact with the wider Church. This, I would argue, is something that lies at the heart of the New Evangelisation: the act of reaching out to those who have, for any number of reasons, lost touch with the Church. Whether seeking the assistance of chaplains and clergy to contribute expertise within the RE class, to support the further development of staff knowledge or confidence, or provide opportunity to encounter the sacraments in the life of school, there are innumerable instances in which the role of communicator between parents and families can be realised through the unique role of the RE teacher. And for those students who are not Catholics, this approach, at the very least, provides them with a greater awareness of the wider community of which they are a part.

Unique Schools

To speak of the unique nature of Catholic education, and therefore, Catholic schools and RE teachers, is not intended to create bipartisan sentiment, nor feed a ghettoised understanding of any given Catholic community. We should feel compelled to rearticulate unapologetically the distinctiveness of all these constituent parts of the Catholic school project, especially in a culture characterised by a reluctance to identify formally with anything. To do this, we need to know and understand the role of RE teachers within this mission. We cannot commit to something we have not been formed in and we cannot expect all those relied upon to bring the Church's educational mission to fruition to do so without being conscious of the task at hand, and being adequately sustained for the journey. All of this, of course, necessitates a self-awareness resulting in a commitment to continue to grow in our faith and understanding as well as our responsibility to recognise which aspects of our professional development as Catholic teachers, but also specifically as RE teachers, we need to address.

We must understand that the Catholic vision of education flows from our unique vision of the human person as made in the image and likeness of God. It is not a reductionist but a holistic approach to forming the whole person. We promote the pursuit of knowledge and truth as a virtuous enterprise with the result that learning is not limited to what is important according to economic or social demands and is not just about skills for the labour market; it is also about self-improvement, self-education and the common good. Learning should encompass everything, including the wonder and majesty of God, and it is this Christian anthropology that prevents us from becoming commodities.

It is clear then that as a Church we are fully committed to the formation of the whole person in order that they be at the service of the common good and not merely be 'useful' people. This is a message that is both applicable and beneficial to every young person in our Catholic schools regardless of faith background. Creating opportunities to encounter the person of Jesus Christ must be the centre of every educational experience and He must remain an example and inspiration to all who are in His service in our schools.

Cardinal Grocholewski describes his understanding of some of the troubles marking schools:

> Education is also suffering from evils afflicting our societies: widespread subjectivism, moral relativism and nihilism. Schools are often asked to be merely instructive, that is, capable of providing cognitive instruments and of making 'human resources' 'function' in the complex economic system of our world.[4]

Not everyone involved in education would recognise these characteristics as entirely negative. However, for Catholic schools they represent a wider agenda that seeks to re-define the very nature of the human person which can never co-exist within a Catholic vision of education. However distinct the foundational aims and approaches of denominational institutions may be from non-denominational, the fact is that the same is expected of both in a state-funded system, with the consequence that we must re-sell the Church's educational mission to each new generation. With this comes the realisation that our RE teachers are very often the first port of call in this activity.

Any response to this changing landscape or to the challenges of the New Evangelisation which does not clearly identify and articulate what we are about as Catholic educational institutions will be lost amongst the many relativistic approaches and deafening neo-positivistic views that dominate our culture. The effectiveness of our response will rely upon strong leadership at every level, not least from classroom teachers, who, through their witness and relationships, have the potential to effect important change in the lives of our young people.

Teachers as Agents of the New Evangelisation

Catholic teaching must be identifiable by its vocational nature. It can never be one job choice amongst many but rather it is a personal response to serve Christ and the Church. Even if every teacher is not able to articulate it in this fashion, or is even conscious that their becoming a teacher was directed by the hand of providence, it is a response to a call or it cannot be described as a vocation. Nonetheless, we will all have had different formative experiences and with this comes a variety of understandings on the role of the Catholic RE teacher and a variety of levels of formation and knowledge gained from family, parish, schools and universities. If the intended recipients of the New Evangelisation initiatives are secularised or disassociated Catholics and the school is, for many, where their only encounter with the Church occurs, then we need to be sure that those teachers who are the front line of this mission have the necessary opportunities to realise their full potential. What is certain is that 'one can only hand on that which one has first received.'[5]

Regardless of which subject area a teacher may be specialised in, all are called to facilitate the permeation of the Catholic ethos in every area of the school. My own subject specialisation is RE and I am often envious of how much more convincing someone from another subject is able to be in matters of faith. My own experience is that students expect certain behaviours and attitudes from the RE specialist teacher which when delivered by another subject teacher, seem novel, attractive and more reasonable. Whatever the reasons for this frustrating phenomenon may be, it should be noted that teachers from other subject areas have the potential to be credible and effective witnesses to students in a unique way. Teaching outwith a formal association with RE, they have the capacity to make present an integrated vision of a lived faith. And this is why they, above all, need solid formation in the educational mission of the Church and continued renewal throughout their careers.

Furthermore, as effective agents of the New Evangelisation, teachers need to be aware that our unique identity as Catholic teachers in Catholic schools is not something that can be compartmentalised. We do not become distinct because we are Catholic teachers; we are distinct because of the unity of the Catholic vision which necessarily influences every area of our lives. If we are not proponents of an integrated Catholicism we cannot witness to an integrated Catholicism to our students, and it is this overarching unity of belief, worship and life that transcends subject boundaries:

> For the Catholic Educator, whatever is true is a participation in Him who is the Truth; the communication of truth, therefore, as a professional activity, is thus fundamentally transformed into a unique participation in the prophetic mission of Christ, carried on through one's teaching.[6]

The sentiment behind this is transformative for all educators. It recognises that it is not only when you are formally teaching RE in class that you participate in the mission of Christ. Any given specialisation is about communicating truth, beauty and goodness, with the result that whenever you bring a student closer to truth, beauty and goodness, you bring them closer to God, regardless of the subject. Teaching students the laws of physics is teaching them about the truth of the universe, which is teaching them about God. Exploring the human condition through poetry in English is bringing students closer to understanding their relationship with their creator and the world around them. In order to appreciate fully this unity we must be careful to avoid creating dualisms between subject areas. Learning about God, in the broadest definition, cannot be limited to one subject area, just as evangelising in our schools cannot be restricted to the RE curriculum. What this understanding allows RE teachers to do is utilise the many different talents and creative abilities of teachers of other subject specialisations to enliven and re-invigorate the teaching of RE both in a broad sense which sees the Catholic ethos permeating every area of the curriculum and also in the teaching of RE in a formal sense. Because of the all-encompassing nature of RE it is tempting to think that the RE teacher's role is always to provide for non-specialists, from the day to day provision of resources to the accompaniment of these teachers in the delivery of RE. However, I think this outlook provides us with an opportunity to reflect upon what we can gain from non-specialist teachers in terms of approach and pedagogy and a unique perspective on cross-curricular links with our own subject.

None of these observations should detract from the fact that RE as a distinct curricular area should be subject to the same rigour applied to any other area of the curriculum. So too should the resourcing and teaching of RE be comparable to every other area of the school. The catechetical nature brought to teaching RE by a practising Catholic is essential but should always exist alongside and be interwoven with an academic understanding of the subject at hand. Recognising that there is a body of knowledge to be communicated and learned should be the foundation of any subject.

Unified Learning

Segregation of learning about religion from learning and knowledge as a unitive approach to understanding impoverishes any educational mission. It would change the holistic approach to the transmission of the faith that is facilitated by this approach. Owing to the fact that schools are very often microcosms of society, this separation echoes the further reaching and more damaging version of secularism that dominates in many places. When religion is separated from everything else, just as we do when we separate RE as a subject from all other areas of the school:

> religion becomes one more department of human life, one activity among others ... [with the result that] only a religion which is a way of living in every sphere either deserves or can hope to survive. For the task of religion is to help see the secular as the sacred, the world as under God.[7]

Whether as an RE teacher or as a teacher of another discipline, we must realise that: 'the catechetical mission of the school does not exist solely with the RE syllabus.'[8] Of course, the curricular expectations placed on the RE teacher will be different from that of a Maths or Drama teacher, but the task of educating young people in the faith should be realised by all staff in every area of the school. In this way, it is too limiting to describe the mission of a Catholic educator with the single word 'teacher' and entirely fitting, given that we teach not only through our subjects but also what we say and how we live our vocation, to describe us as catechists.

Creative Agents of the Divine Pedagogy

Recognising the inherent catechetical nature of our vocation, we take as our authority and example the Divine Pedagogy: the way that God teaches us about Himself through Divine Revelation. God is the ultimate teacher and it is from him that we receive our call and mandate as *catechists* and against him that all forms of pedagogy must be measured. Just as authentic Christian education encourages personal encounter with the person of Christ, so too living the vocation to teach demands daily renewal of our commitment. This positive and recurring decision is the mark of any vocation but our position as RE teachers gives us unique opportunities in which to engage students with the beauty of the faith: 'by sharing the same form of life as those whom they catechise, lay catechists have a special sensitivity for incarnating the Gospel in the concrete life of men and women.'[9] As lay people who have responded to a call to teach, we have unlimited potential to positively demonstrate how to live the Catholic faith in everyday situations and within the RE classroom we experience daily, if not hourly, occasions in which to witness to this. When what we believe is so often counter-cultural, this can lend a much needed air of accessibility to the faith for young people. If they see their teachers as being faithful in the world then they will feel strengthened in their own potential to become committed and articulate Catholics who know, understand, love and live what it means to be Catholic.

The way we teach as well as what we teach is how God's pedagogy is made known. We are 'the means by which the divine pedagogy continues and is effectively present.'[10] We are not simply repeating or imitating an action of God isolated to certain times in history but are instead dynamic instruments of his continued presence amongst us. Catholic teaching is often referred to as an experience of spiritual mother or fatherhood and this description goes a long way to articulating what is meant by *in loco parentis*. In the same way that we would recognise parents as co-creators when they cooperate with God in being open to children, as teachers we contribute to the ongoing formation of that young person and, therefore, play an important part in the continuation of that creative action of God in the way that we execute our role as catechists.

A lived faith relies upon a fruitful relationship with the Church and the nature of the Church means we have daily opportunities to meet Christ in the sacraments; we are taught, nourished, and renewed by him through them. Given that in many situations, teachers represent the only link with the institutional Church, it is of fundamental importance that we stay close to Christ through his Church and make her as necessary and as alive to the young people in front of us as she is in our own lives.

Teaching a Culture

Renewing the Catholic culture of our schools is our best hope as teachers of being effective agents of the New Evangelisation, but this is something which cannot be left solely to the RE department. No teacher has ever graduated with all the knowledge and pedagogical skills needed to be a teacher of any subject. As professionals, we accept that becoming a skilled teacher is the result of a commitment to life-long professional development and our attitude towards becoming a skilled and knowledgeable catechist should reflect the same professional rigour. Education in the faith, if it is something we have not been fortunate enough to have received in our formative years, needs to be something that we learn for ourselves and then transmit. But, differently from the students in our care, we have the ability to self-direct our study and the necessary academic discipline to be effective independent learners. A good teacher will always evaluate the successes and areas for development of their students as well as themselves and our approach and engagement with the New Evangelisation would benefit from the same kind of honest appraisal which seeks to always improve on what has gone before to expand our capacity to evangelise.

The enormity of the task of the New Evangelisation should not be intimidating to us either as school communities of faith and learning or as individual RE teachers and all should be aware of and strengthened in their own power to effect positive change. As St Thérèse says: 'Do small things with great love.' Every act of witness that we engage in as teachers has the potential to enhance the faith of the young people in our care and bring them closer in relationship with Christ. To be sure, this is a responsibility of great magnitude but is not something to be feared. Teachers should be supported in their efforts by parents first and foremost and by the Church through school chaplains and Bishops, Diocesan education departments and Catholic teacher education institutions as well as national educational bodies and the many Catholic charitable organisations that work with our schools. This support should be characterised by frequent communication between parties and a variety of accessible opportunities for professional and personal development that at all times respects and complements the vocational and catechetical nature of the Catholic teacher. Catholic teachers cannot be asked to do that which they are not supported and renewed in and those responsible for the formation of teachers need to provide the highest standard of Catholic vocational development opportunities possible.

We should, however, accept that the transformation required by the New Evangelisation will not happen overnight but will be the result of a 'long-term embedding of the faith in culture.'[11] This task will necessarily require the active co-operation of all. It will begin with a recognition of our distinct nature as Catholic educational establishments and should affect everything from the values and virtues that form any given school's mission statement to the charities that we support and the dinner hall menu on a Friday in Lent.

The difference between teaching students about religion and allowing them to share and develop a lived faith will be the difference between the success or failure of the part we play as teachers in the New Evangelisation. However advanced resources that aid teaching become, they will never replace the teacher and this is even more true when we understand that being a Catholic teacher, and specifically an RE teacher, is synonymous with being a witness to the faith.

And this applies to both staff and students. In our role as RE teachers, we should recognise our own areas of specialism and seek ways in which to provide opportunities for development to non-specialist teachers. We should rise to the challenge of presenting the best version of a lived vocation to the young people in our care and this commitment should be present in every area of our lives, as well as every area of the school. A Catholic teacher who witnesses to his or her faith day after day, even in the smallest of ways, will be infinitely more effective in bringing young people to Christ than someone who merely knows how to teach something well. This is the real challenge and opportunity that the New Evangelisation affords the Catholic RE teacher.

Notes

1   J. M. Unger, *Evangelisation* (Archdiocese of St Louis, Catholic Education Office). Available at: http://archstl.org/education/page/ evangelization.

2   Pope John Paul II, *Redemptoris Missio (7 December 1990)*, 3.

3   See T. Rowland, 'Catholic Education as a Theological Project', p. 14 above.

4   Z. Grocholewski, *Mission of Catholic Schools for Evangelization today* (2002).

5   P. de Cointet, B. Morgan, and P. Willey, *The Catechism of the Catholic Church and the Craft of Catechesis, [with introductory essay by Christoph Cardinal Schönborn]* (San Francisco: Ignatius Press, 2008), p. 15.

6   Sacred Congregation for Catholic Education, *Lay Catholics in schools: Witnesses to faith.* (1982), 10.

7   A. C. MacIntyre, *Marxism: An Interpretation* (London: SCM Press, 1953), p. 9 as quoted by Rowland in the present volume.

8   R. Convery, L. Franchi, R. McCluskey, *Reclaiming the Piazza: Catholic Education as a Cultural Project* (Leominster: Gracewing, 2014), p. 17.

9   Congregation for the Clergy, *General Directory for Catechesis* (1996), 230.

10   C. Farey, W. Linnig and M. J. Paruch (eds.), *The Pedagogy of God: Its Centrality in Catechesis and Catechist Formation* (Steubenville: Emmaus Road Publishing), p. 3.

11   De Cointet et al., *Catechism of the Catholic Church and the Craft of Catechesis*, p. 23.

Social Media: The Word Made Digital Dwells Amongst Us

Ronnie Convery

I N THE DYING days of the dramatic decade that was the 1970s, a song topped the charts across Europe and the United States which may have seemed like a betrayal and provocation to educators of good will.

Pink Floyd's rare foray into the singles charts with *Another Brick in the Wall* circled and re-circled round the fearful lines, 'We don't need no education, we don't need no thought control ...' The music was as engaging as the message was threatening.

Almost 40 years later the episode is worth recalling, for it speaks of a world that is no more. Today's educators must surely be glad of its passing. The song's protagonist speaks of having a personal wall around him sealing him off from the rest of the world; teachers were 'Just another brick in that wall'. Today, in no small measure through the use of social media, that wall has been well and truly demolished.

Learning to Adapt

Throughout history, educational systems have had to adapt to changes in culture and wider society. The passage from the quill to the fountain pen must have seemed revolutionary; the arrival of the biro with the concomitant redundancy for rather splendid little ink wells sunk into school desks must have taken a little getting used to; the arrival of the pocket calculator must have seemed a mortal threat to arithmeticians of the old school and the advent of the PC must surely have required a dramatic change of mindset from all those involved in the imparting of knowledge.

However, it is perhaps in our own day that the greatest challenge is placed before the educator (and evangeliser) with the advent of social media. For some it is an enemy to be kept at the gates, for others a risk to be managed, but for educators with an eye on history it must surely be seen as a gift to be welcomed, though with due prudence and careful management, into the educational experience of 21st century humanity.

Social Media: A Reality Check

The truth is that educators and all involved in the communication of a message have no choice but to adapt to social media. It exists. It impacts. It affects the learning and life experience of every student and every educator — whether they have a Facebook page of their own or not; whether they tweet hourly, annually or never. Social media are not like electronic comics which can be kept outside the lecture room door; neither are they like water pistols which can be confiscated or advertising campaigns which can be ignored. Examples of social media are present in every classroom, every lecture hall, every learning suite, just as surely as hydrogen and oxygen.

It is essential for all involved in cultural engagement to be sensitive to this reality. Even those not directly participating in networks of communication must be aware of the impact such networks have on the surrounding culture, on the way people consume and process information and on the whole concept of education. Any educator trying to turn back the cultural waves unleashed by the advent of social media will fail just as spectacularly as Canute once failed to convince the waters to retreat from his increasingly wet feet.

It is interesting to note that one of the world's most traditional institutions, one which is sometimes unfairly attacked for its slowness to adapt to change, is open and indeed enthusiastic in its embrace of the possibilities opened by social media. Pope Francis used his *World Communications Day Message* in January 2016 to state:

> Emails, text messages, social networks and chats can
> also be fully human forms of communication. It is

> not technology which determines whether or not communication is authentic, but rather the human heart and our capacity to use wisely the means at our disposal. Social networks can facilitate relationships and promote the good of society, but they can also lead to further polarization and division between individuals and groups. The digital world is a public square, a meeting-place where we can either encourage or demean one another, engage in a meaningful discussion or unfair attacks.[1]

This quote is backed up by actions. The Pontiff's Twitter account, every tweet of which is seen and approved by the Pope himself, has around 10 million followers in the English version alone. Add to that 12 million in Spanish, 4 million in Italian, 2.5 million in Portuguese and even 700,000 in Latin! This leads to an important, indeed urgent question: Why does an institution so institutionally conservative but also inherently educative, use social media?

Antonio Spadaro SJ, Editor of the Jesuit journal *La Civiltà Cattolica*, sees clearly the 'digital imperative':

> I'm not so much interested in offering answers about whether the Internet is good or bad (it's not inherently either) or what it does to the nature and quality of your social life… we need a shift in how we think about the Net in general. By nature, it's a network, not a physical reality; moreover, it's a network with access to lots of things—some good, some not so good. We've got to get away from moralizing about the Net to thinking about how to use it and towards thinking about how to live in the time of the Net.[2]

Spadaro acknowledges head-on the fear of many educators that the Web in general, and social media in particular, will undermine the educator's authority:

> The theory and nature of authority… There's no central power or mediator on the Net, as the common example of online news consumption highlights. Instead of leaving judgment of the slant

and veracity of an article to a professional editor or
producer, many people now produce and "edit"
their own news sources. In that environment, how
do we decide (and who decides?) which source(s) of
content are considered trusted and authoritative,
and why? We're starting to see the same questions
popping up in real-life spirituality, too: when people
can search out and find whatever texts, theories or
practices they want, that pretty clearly changes the
relationship they have with liturgy and the Word.

For Spadaro, social media are not only not a threat, but
should be seen as an educational tool. He compares social
media engagement to the *Spiritual Exercises* proposed by St
Ignatius of Loyola:

You go deeper not by hearing or reading some Scripture and silently pondering it but by being asked to
imagine yourself in the Bible stories and in fact speaking with (colloquy) the characters. That's very much
the way in which people approach online thought
(read/watch, leave comment, post to share site).

If it is clear that social networks are here to stay, what
lessons must be borne in mind for those who wish to use
them effectively? There follow some suggestions.

The first requirement is to know one's audience. It
simply will not do to declare that one is communicating
with 'everyone' for to do so is to be so hopelessly unfocused
that one communicates rather with 'no-one'. Given the
enormity of the web, the understandable fear of speaking
to a small constituency can be forgotten. Some of the most
effective evangelisation on the web comes from a clearly
focused but well-thought out stream.

One only has to look at the enormous success of the
blogs/social media presence/books/events of the Italian
journalist, Costanza Miriano, to understand that quality
insight, well presented, with a touch of daring originality
will have a massive impact. Worldwide book sales of her
deliberately provocatively titled *Marry Him and Be Submis-*

sive stand at over 200,000.[3] (In Italy a book is considered a success if it sells more than 3000, but this title is now translated into Spanish, French, German, Dutch, English and Polish too.) With blog visits into the millions, a Facebook Page that is closed to new 'friends' having reached the maximum possible number of followers allowed by the platform, it can be deduced that depth rather than breadth is important in communicating a clear message. Given that her online 'persona' appears somewhat specialised in its reach: ie Italian native speaking women of devout Catholic faith, under 50, with children, working and juggling child care issues, interested in saints and indulgences but also fashion and pop music, devoted to the Madonna but also the latest line in designer handbags, with a sense of humour and relationship worries, guilt feelings about being a bad cook and a sense of injustice about the lack of fair treatment for women in the workplace, a penchant for religious jewellery and a childlike piety (a fairly precise demographic!) it can be seen that success does not require a blunderbuss approach to communication attempting to reach 'everyone'.

But beware. Defining an audience is not a matter of excluding, but rather including. Miriano's success is that she manages to 'hook' those who may not share her religious outlook through humour, or through a social agenda or through references to everyday life that ring true for persons of almost all walks of life. Thus the reader is introduced gradually to a fairly traditional form of Catholicism, through an unlikely route. This point is key: social media must be seen as the route to the destination and not the destination itself.

Social media should be seen as a form of digitally tapping people on the shoulder at the bus stop and saying 'Have you seen this?' The 'this' may be a bible verse or a job advert; a thought for the day or an inspiring book review. The destination will vary, but the route is social media.

Many educational institutions are already implementing social media marketing successfully as a tool for recruiting new students. Those who are wise will be using it as a platform to talk about the success of current students and perhaps how the school is improving all the time. Their digital outreach will be bait, not a three course meal!

In a school setting, digital communication can have multiple practical uses. Some of these (though by no means an exhaustive list) are listed below.

Social Media in the Classroom

In this section I offer some practical suggestions re the use of social media in the classroom.

- **Classroom Blogs**: The idea here is that each class has their own blog which is managed by the teacher but authored by the students. The pupil who generates the most interesting essay or paper on the topic of that week will have his/her work published online to the classroom blog. This will give those chosen a huge sense of achievement and, hopefully, inspire the other students in the class to work harder to achieve online publication. To take this a step further, you could also add a friendly level of competition by having classes compete.

- **Video Learning**: Old people love video, young people love video—this cannot be argued as *YouTube* is the world's third most visited site. Video should be used more in school and if these videos were posted to a class YouTube account, then the students could re-watch the videos at home whilst doing their homework!

- **Teacher Twitter Accounts**: There is an invisible barrier between a teacher and their students, the great teachers smash through that. Most of us remember teachers who were somehow 'present' to us. 3D figures with real life opinions and defects, with first names and families, not 2D caricatures in a gown and mortarboard. It could be argued that teachers having their own teacher Twitter account would take a big leap into removing some of the bricks in humanising and personalising learning. Educators could post lesson summaries answer homework questions, or even have students tweet what they have learned in 140 characters to the teacher account! This will allow the students to feel much more connected to their teacher and remind them that their teacher is actually a real person with an interesting message and knowledge package to deliver.

- **Fake Accounts:** There is a common assumption that since today's students are often perceived to be digital natives, educators must find ways to introduce digital language and methodology into their teaching. Classes that are covering historical figures can use social media to really get into the life of that person. An insightful educator will have students create a Facebook account on a piece of paper for the historical figures they are considering. Putting all of their likes, interests, some status updates etc. On the other hand care must be exercised lest pupils abuse the means, and indulge in unsavoury, unhelpful and, ultimately, useless digital excursions.

Social Media as Educator in Life Skills

There are those who lament that social media has dealt a death blow to grammar and syntax. Text messages (SMS) with their useful, though annoying abbreviations, bleed into everyday written communications. Thus abbreviations such as LOL, IMHO and BYOB are just as likely to be seen in emails, and even some print publications as they are on smart phone screens. But just as nature evolves, so does language, and it could be argued that digital communication is the most powerful driving force in modern linguistic development.[4]

However, social media also require an age old skill, one beloved of old-school grammarians. Facebook, but especially Twitter, require extraordinary powers of summarisation to be used effectively. Twitter limits posts to 140 characters, but studies show that using all the characters available is a mistake. It is generally believed that 71-to-100 characters is a good guideline. What makes this length optimal? Tweets at this length get more retweets. They also have higher reply rate, retweet rate, and combined reply/retweet rate. Studies have found the 100-character mark to be the sweet spot for tweet length. Track Social studied 100 major brands (Oreo, Zappos, ESPN, etc.) for a 30-day period in autumn 2012. Buddy Media studied 320 Twitter handles from major brands for two-and-a-half months at the beginning of 2012 and both studies concurred in their findings.[5]

Surprisingly,Facebook posts do best when they are shorter even than Twitter posts! Maximum engagement happens here at just 40 characters and engagement slowly wanes the longer you go on after this point. An 80-character post is better than 100-character post. A 40-character post is better than 80. What makes this length optimal? Posts at this length tend to receive a higher 'like' rate, comment rate, and combined like/comment rate (statistics that include a comparison of total engagement to number of Facebook fans.) Where does this data come from? Again two studies found that shorter is better on Facebook. A Buddy Media study of the top 100 retailers' Facebook pages during a six-month period in 2011 is one of the most-cited sources. Also in 2011, BlitzLocal studied 11,000 Facebook pages over a seven-month period (ibid.)

If social media can be harnessed as an aid to a vital communication skill, namely summarising, can it be seen as useful training in other areas of life? Italian journalist and academic, Bruno Mastroianni, speaks powerfully of the potential of social media to break down barriers and facilitate dialogue. For Mastroianni, the world of digital communication is simply an extension of inter-personal dialogue.⁶ Insults traded on Twitter are merely the insults traded in the street in written form, according to the Rome-based lecturer. Moreover, the human skills needed for survival in the world of work can, according to him, be learned online, on screen, on a smart phone.

In a recent speech to European communicators, Mastroianni described how to win over potential enemies, and avoid entrenchment into the ever tempting digital bunker.⁷ He highlights two key rules which are as valid for daily as they are for digital life:

1.   Do not speak only to those who share your own views. To do so is tempting, for sure. One's beliefs are fortified, one's fear disappears and one's ego is massaged. But to what end? To preach to the converted is a fool's game—at best a waste of time, at worst a form of self-delusion. Too often digital communicators—ie everyone who uses social media—operate in what Mastroianni calls 'echo-chambers' where their own views echo and return louder than ever because the audience to which they broadcast (or better the individuals with whom they dialogue) share their own premises. Moral of the story? Be brave! Dare to follow online those whose views you may not share … for it is only by knowing what other people think and write that you can gauge your own views and beliefs, test the strength of your own arguments (or prejudices) and engage in dialogue.

2.   Do not resort to entrenchment. By this Mastroianni means, do not respond to barriers of opinion by trying to bulldozer the barrier out of the way. The more one tries to force one's interlocutor into submission, the more the interlocutor digs in, reinforcing the wall of incomprehension and making any prospect of meaningful engagement, let alone mutual enrichment, remote to say the

least. Instead, Mastroianni calls for a new approach. When faced with a wall—he urges—do not try to knock it down, but rather try to go round the side of it, seeking out the 'opponent' where he or she is. For the Italian academic it is essential to meet the person we are trying to engage with, and perhaps open to new horizons, on their home territory. There, we can look at a problem from their perspective, and use our imagination to discover approaches which will work given the individual set of factors which shape the world view of our interlocutor.

These rules surely apply as life skills too. The old joke that Christ sought out fishers of men, not keepers of aquariums, is as true now as ever; indeed in the polarised world of social media the truth of the phrase deserves to be constantly recalled.

The Imperative of Social Media

For the modern teacher, preacher, educator, communicator, indeed for the engaged human being of the early 21st century, social media are no longer an optional extra. Communication happens on social media. It has become not only the fastest deliverer of information but also the first recipient of that information.

There was also a tipping point in 2013 that has major implications for businesses and for the Church. This point will impact publishing and marketing and evangelising strategies and tactics in the future.

That year on 13 December, Beyoncé, one of the world's most successful music stars ignored the traditional mass media product launching process of a radio campaign, multiple TV appearances and retail and consumer brand promotions and so on which are the usual requirement for successful album sales.

Instead she announced her new album on Instagram with just a picture, captioned 'Surprise!'. Amazingly, this one picture sent the music world into instantaneous melt-down. What she did was release her new album on iTunes without warning. An Instagram post was all she needed. Twitter reported a whopping 1.2 million tweets about the album in just 12 hours and the new album sold 828,773 copies in just three days, making it i-Tunes's fastest-selling album worldwide.

Two years later in the hours following the election of Donald Trump as President of the United States, long before he gave his first interview or delivered his first policy address, he used Twitter to speak to the world. A similar technique was used by outgoing president, Barack Obama. Twitter had gone from being a platform which reported news, to being the platform making news. Stories which once featured in newspaper headlines before being tweeted, now feature on tweets before becoming newspaper headlines. These new forms of behaviour are posing an immense challenge and are also providing great opportunities to the Church and the proclamation of her message. Church teaching has not changed but the people called to accept and interiorise and proclaim that tradition are living in a new world.

Professor Raphael Monthienvichienchai, speaking to the World Congress on the New Evangelisation in Rome in 2014 put it like this: 'As Christians, we are not called to just invite people into the Church; but also to bring the Church to the people.'[8]

The Second Vatican Council, in one of the first decrees issued by the Council Fathers, *Inter Mirifica*, states:

> Among the wonderful technological discoveries which men of talent, especially in the present era, have made with God's help, the Church welcomes and promotes with special interest those which have … uncovered new avenues of communicating… news, views and teachings of every sort. The most important of these inventions are media such as the press, movies, radio, television and the like. These can … reach and influence, not only individuals, but the very masses and the whole of human society…[9]

Today that text would surely place in first position, in terms of influence on people's lives, social media. As Professor Monthienvichienchai states:

> Social media has become the nervous system of our new culture, in which more and more people are expressing and exploring their identity, picking up and discarding their values and attitudes, expressing their feelings and prejudices, befriending and unfriending each other, measuring each other's status and importance, relevance and appearance. If our young people and people of all ages are living in this gigantic network, then we, as people of faith need to be in there, interacting with the inhabitants of this world, with the men and women who dwell in the social media.

When we speak about new evangelisation in the Church, we more often than not think of the so called 'real world', but billions of people live in the social networks. These have been described as among the biggest countries in the world — and they are countries with no barriers. For example, more than 1.2 billion inhabit the world of Facebook. The majority of these people may never enter a Church, but if we are to respond to the Gospel mandate given us by Christ to 'go out to the whole world', then we must include the digital world and proclaim the Good News there also. Our challenge as evangelisers has always been to reach out and encounter people wherever they are — and increasingly that means going online.

We used to ask ourselves, 'What do we need to tell people?' Now we also have to ask ourselves, 'What do people want to hear from us?' and 'How do people want to hear from us?' They no longer want to wait for the evening newscast, or the morning paper, or even the Sunday homily. If we do not go to them, they will go elsewhere.[10]

Concluding Remarks

Jacques Buguin recently wrote a summary article for McKinseys, the global management consultant firm, aimed at getting a sharper, commercial sense of how social media affected consumer choice. The concluding words of his article deserve to be printed and framed and set above the desk of every communicator, teacher and preacher:

> The pathways of social influence are shifting constantly. Looking ahead, better mobile devices and more robust social applications will make it even easier to share experiences about products and services. Companies can't afford to fall behind this powerful curve.[11]

If that advice is relevant for marketers and manufacturers, how much more true must it be for those trading in ideas and knowledge? The challenge will be to stay true to one's guiding principles while expressing those ideas in a language that is new, in a format that is different, and in a context which is constantly changing. Reclaiming the piazza for justice, truth and dignity will become increasingly a digital challenge. It is a task in which today's educator, communicator and evangeliser must engage.

Notes

[1]   Pope Francis, *Message for World Day of Communications*, 2016.

[2]   Berkley Center for Religion, Peace and World Affairs, *A Conversation with Antonio Spadaro SJ, Journalist at Civilta Cattolica Review, Rome*, 2012. Available at: https://berkleycenter.georgetown.edu/interviews/a-conversation-with-antonio-spadaro-sj-journalist-at-civilta-cattolica-review-rome.

[3]   C. Miriano, *Sposati e sii Sottomessa* (Venice: Sonsongo, 2012).

[4]   N. Baron, *Are Digital Media Changing Language?* 2009. Available at: http://www.ascd.org/publications/educational-leadership/mar09/vol66/num06/Are-Digital-Media-Changing-Language%C2%A2.aspx.

5   K. Lee, *Infographic: The Optimal Length for Every Social Media Update and More*, 2016. Available at: https://blog.bufferapp.com/optimal-length-social-media.

6   Catholic Bishops Conference of Europe, *Communications Commission Conference*, Glasgow, November 2016.

7   *Ibid.*

8   R. Monthienvichienchai, *New Evangelisation and Social Media*, 2014. Available at: http://www.novaevangelizatio.va/content/nvev/en/eventi/Incontro-evangelii-gaudium/relazioni-incontro-internazionale/prof-chainarong-monthienvichienchai.pdf.

9   Second Vatican Council, Decree *Inter Mirifica*, 1.

10   Monthienvichienchai, *New Evangelisation and Social Media*.

11   J. Bughin, Getting A Sharper Picture of Social Media's Influence, 2016. Available at: http://www.mckinsey.com/business-functions/marketing-and-sales/our-insights/getting-a-sharper-picture-of-social-medias-influence.

CONTRIBUTORS

ISABELLE BOYD is well-known across the Scottish Education community with over 20 years' experience in senior leadership. She is a Chief Officer in a local authority having previously served as Headteacher for 11 years. Cardinal Newman High School achieved an excellent HMIe report in 2008. The areas judged to be excellent included leadership and developing people and partnerships. However, the most professionally satisfying comment was 'The school was very successful in taking forward its vision of making a significant difference to the life choices of its pupils.' Isabelle has a national profile and is invited to serve on working groups, address conferences and write for a variety of media. She was seconded by Scottish Government to set up a Scottish College for Educational Leadership. She was an executive member of Catholic Headteachers Association of Scotland for 8 years and served as national Chair from 2010–12. Isabelle was awarded a CBE for Services to Education in 2008. The honour not only reflects well on her but on Catholic Education in Scotland and endorses HMIe's findings that she 'provided outstanding leadership'.

FRANCIS CAMPBELL joined the Foreign and Commonwealth office as a member of HM Diplomatic Service in 1997. From 1999 to 2003 Francis served on the staff of Prime Minister Tony Blair, and from 2005 to 2011 he served as Her Majesty's Ambassador to the Holy See. In 2014 he was appointed as the Vice-Chancellor of St Mary's University, Twickenham, London and he has recently overseen the launch of Vision 2025, which outlines St Mary's plan for the future. Francis is a Member of the Advisory Panel of the Independent Anti-Slavery Commissioner, is a governor of St Mary's University, St Elizabeth's School, Richmond and Carlow College, Ireland. He is a Trustee of St Joseph's Hospice, Hackney and Forward Thinking a London based NGO and think-tank. He is a regular contributor to Radio 4's Thought for the Day and a columnist for *The Tablet* magazine.

RONNIE CONVERY is a journalist who has written for many titles in the UK and Italy. He is currently Director of Communications for the Archdiocese of Glasgow and Honorary Consul of Italy in the west of Scotland. A graduate of the University of Glasgow he has also studied at Università La Sapienza in Rome and the Institut de Touraine in France. He is a regular broadcaster on issues related to faith, politics and culture and has pioneered the use of social media by religious organisations. He has given guest lectures on the topic in Scotland and Italy. He edited the tribute volume, *The Cardinal* published following the death of Cardinal Thomas Winning in 2001 and was co-author of *Reclaiming the Piazza: Catholic Education as a Cultural Project* in 2014. He was named a Cavaliere of the Italian Republic by President Giorgio Napolitano in 2008 in recognition of services to Italian culture and community.

ARCHBISHOP LEO WILLIAM CUSHLEY is the Archbishop and Metropolitan of St Andrews & Edinburgh in Scotland. Born in 1961 in Wester Moffat, Lanarkshire, he was educated at Holy Cross High School, Hamilton (1973–1975) before going onto junior seminary at St Mary's College, Blairs (1975–1979) and then the Pontifical Scots College, Rome (1979–1987). He was ordained to the priesthood on 7 July 1985 by the Right Reverend Joseph Devine, Bishop of Motherwell. The immediately subsequent years saw him serve as both assistant priest and school chaplain within various Lanarkshire communities. In 1994 he was asked to join the Holy See's diplomatic service which led to three years of studies at the Pontifical Ecclesiastical Academy in Rome (1994–1997). Postings then followed to Burundi (1997–2001); Portugal (2001–2004); The United Nations, New York (2004–2007); South Africa, Lesotho, Namibia, Swaziland (2007–2008); adding to them Botswana (2008–2009).

In 2009 he was appointed Head of English Language Section within the Secretariat of State of the Vatican, a post he held until 2013 when His Holiness Pope Francis nominated him as Archbishop and Metropolitan of St Andrews & Edinburgh. He was consecrated by Cardinal James Harvey at St Mary's Metropolitan Cathedral in Edinburgh on 21 September 2013, the feast of St Matthew the Apostle. Archbishop Cushley is a graduate of the Pontifical Gregorian University, Rome (PhB 1981; STB 1984; JCD 1997) and the Sant'Anselmo Pontifical Liturgical Institute, Rome (SLL 1987).

NATALIE FINNIGAN studied Theology at the University of Glasgow. She had a particular interest in bioethics and dedicated her final year's dissertation to a study which looked at HIV prevention and the Catholic vision. Natalie then completed PGDE with a specialism in Religious Education and spent seven years working as an RE teacher in St John Ogilvie High School in Lanarkshire. In 2014 she became the Religious Education Adviser for Secondary Schools for the Archdiocese of Glasgow. This position involves day to day support of Principal Teachers of Religious Education, creating and delivering CLPL courses for Catholic teachers and teachers working in Catholic schools and supporting and advising senior management in the twenty-one High Schools across the Archdiocese as well as working collaboratively on a national level with other diocesan advisers, The Scottish Education Service and the University of Glasgow.

LEONARDO FRANCHI is a member of the School of Education at the University of Glasgow. He has many years experience of teaching in schools and universities. He was Director of Catholic Teacher Education at the University of Glasgow from 2012–2016. Leonardo's principal research interests are in the nature of Religious Education and initial teacher education/formation. He has an MA in Modern Languges, an MEd in Religious Education/Catechesis and PhD in

Religious Education. His latest book, *Shared Mission: Religious Education in the Catholic Tradition*, was published in 2016. He has published articles in scholarly journals on a wide range of topics in the field of Catholic education. Leonardo is a member of the Executive of the Association for Catholic Colleges and Institutes of Education (ACISE), the sectorial branch of the International Federation of Catholic Universities and sits on the Executive of the Scottish Catholic Education Service.

BISHOP JOHN KEENAN gained a Law Degree in Forensic Medicine at the University of Glasgow. From there entered seminary in the Pontifical Scots College in Rome, attending the Gregorian University, where he gained a degree in Sacred Theology and a post-graduate in Philosophy with Licence to teach in Catholic institutes and taught Philosophy in the Scottish National Seminary from 1995 to 2005. He was ordained for the Archdiocese of Glasgow and appointed assistant priest at Christ the King Parish, in the south side Kings Park area. From there he was appointed full time chaplain at Holyrood RC Secondary School. In 2000 he was appointed as the Catholic Chaplain at the University of Glasgow by the late Cardinal Winning and in 2014 became the fifth Bishop of Paisley.

FATHER JOSEPH LAPPIN is the Director of the Religious Education Department of the Archdiocese of Glasgow, having obtained a Licence in Sacred Theology, with specialisation in Catechetics, from the Pontifical Salesian University, Rome, in 2001. Prior to his ordination in 2001, he studied at the University of Glasgow and St Andrew's College of Education and worked as a teacher of Religious Education in a Catholic secondary school. Fr Lappin has served as Curate and Parish Priest in several parishes in the Archdiocese of Glasgow and is currently Parish Priest of Our Lady of Good Counsel.

RAYMOND McCLUSKEY studied at the Universities of Glasgow (MA) and Oxford (DPhil). After temporary Lectureships in Medieval History at the Universities of St Andrews and Edinburgh, he completed a PGCE and taught for over a decade in St Aloysius' College, the Jesuit school in Glasgow. In 2004, he joined the Faculty (now School) of Education in the University of Glasgow where he is currently Lecturer in Social Studies (History). He is presently Secretary of the History of Education (UK) Society. Raymond has previously edited *The Scots College, Rome, 1600–2000* (Edinburgh, 2000) and (with Professor Stephen McKinney) *How 'The Teacher' is presented in Literature, History, Religion and the Arts* (Lewiston NY, 2013). A study of two previously neglected late Victorian Catholic poets in Scotland (co-authored with Dr Linden Bicket) features in the 2017 edition of the peer-reviewed journal, *Scottish Literary Review*.

TRACEY ROWLAND holds the St John Paul II Chair of Theology at the University of Notre Dame (Australia). Between 2001– 2017 she was the Dean of the John Paul II Institute for Marriage and Family in Melbourne. She holds two doctorates in theology—the PhD from the Divinity School of Cambridge University and the Pontifical STD from the Lateran University. She also holds degrees in law and philosophy. She is a member of the editorial board of the English language edition of *Communio:International Catholic Review* and a member of the *International Theological Commission*. Her latest books are *Catholic Theology* in Bloomsbury's 'Doing Theology' series, published in 2017, and *The Humanism of the Incarnation: Collected Essays,* published by Emmaus Academic. In 2012 she was awarded the Officer's Cross in the Order of Merit of the Republic of Poland.